The Town on
the Hassayampa

A History of
Wickenburg, Arizona

The Town on the Hassayampa

Mark E. Pry

DESERT CABALLEROS
WESTERN MUSEUM
WICKENBURG, ARIZONA

Desert Caballeros Western Museum

21 North Frontier Street

Wickenburg, Arizona 85390

(520) 684-2272

International Standard Book Number 0-9657377-0-5

Contents

Preface and Acknowledgments / VII

Following the Water as Far as It Goes / 3

The Vulture Mine and the Founding of Wickenburg / 15

The Ups and Downs of a Gold Mining Town / 39

A Mining Community Searches for a New Identity / 57

The Dude Ranch Capital of the World / 89

Tourism and the Growth of Modern Wickenburg / 121

Chronology of Wickenburg History / 143

Suggestions for Further Reading / 147

Index / 153

Credits / 157

Preface and Acknowledgments

FOR MOST AMERICANS, and for more than a few foreign visitors, the basic outline of Arizona history seems familiar enough: first there were Indians and the wilderness, then prospectors and fur trappers, and after them a colorful assortment of soldiers, miners, settlers, frontier merchants, railroad barons, and cowboys. While the cowboys, Indians, and miners provided the local color and excitement, the settlers, merchants, and railroad men built the towns that gradually—but not completely—"civilized" the territory.

Wickenburg has seen all of these figures during the 130-odd years of its history, but it has seen much more as well: guest ranch and resort operators, tourists, highway engineers, real estate developers, and retirees. These additional actors, who are often overlooked when the subject of Arizona's history is raised, belong to the recent past— the period that has seen Arizona transformed from a sparsely populated, largely rural state into one increasingly known for its sprawling cities and rapid growth.

More than anything else, this book has been written to explain how Wickenburg has weathered this transformation. Wickenburg's survival was not always assured, especially after its principal mine, the Vulture, ceased production. However, its residents were able to cultivate new industries—first ranching, then tourism—that allowed the community not only to survive but to prosper. In so doing, they built a town that is as modern as any in Arizona yet also retains visible links to its colorful past, which now is part of the town's commercial appeal.

By necessity this is an interpretive history. Rather than attempt to document every important event and person in the town's past, which would have produced a history too long for anyone except the most dedicated reader, I have chosen to be more selective. The result is a thematic account that, I believe, provides the clearest view of the overall course of Wickenburg's history. It not only explains how the town has (and has not) changed over time; it also places Wickenburg's history in a broader context, showing how events in the Hassayampa River valley often reflected larger forces at work in the American West. Many of the events that took place in Wickenburg—especially the closure of its mines and the arrival of tourists—will be familiar to anyone who has lived in or visited other small towns in the West.

This project has been through several changes since its inception nearly two years ago. Initially the museum planned to publish a book of photographs from its collection. I was hired to help plan the book and do some supplementary research for the photograph captions, which were to provide a brief history of the town from the 1860s up to about the 1950s. However, it soon became apparent that what the museum wanted more than anything else was a narrative history of the town. The museum had already sponsored two books on Wickenburg's past, but they were rather limited in scope: one covered the first twelve years of the town's existence, and the other was a compilation that was more a reference book than anything else. Deciding that an entirely new history of Wickenburg was needed, the museum's History and Research Committee asked me to write one.

In compiling this history, I have incurred some debts that I am now glad to acknowledge. Small-town museums typically do not hire professional historians to write their local histories. That this project was undertaken at all is due to the willingness of the museum's History and Research Committee and Board of Trustees to take on what must have seemed, at the time, a rather ambitious and costly project. In addition to lending their support and enthusiasm, the committee's members—George Bermingham, Elladean Hays Bittner, Julie Macias Brooks, Sandra Kiely, Dallas "Rusty" Gant Jr., Joe Mendelson, Corinne Quayle, and Dora Quesada—also provided many helpful comments and suggestions, especially regarding the selection of photographs. Cheryl Taylor, executive director of the museum while the book was being written, was a model project administrator. She not only helped get the project organized but also gave me virtually a free hand in outlining and writing the history—something that any author who has written a commissioned piece can readily appreciate. Her successor, interim director Myrna Harrison, was equally supportive, providing not only much-needed editorial assistance but also a steady administrative hand while the museum searched for a new director. They and the rest of the museum staff—Sheila Kollasch, Deborah Byrd, and Kathy Wortman—made working at the Desert Caballeros Western Museum a pleasure.

Bruce Dinges and Bob Trennert graciously agreed to read the manuscript while it was in draft, and both provided many helpful comments, with Bruce in particular contributing his sharp eye as an editor. I am especially grateful to my wife, Rose Weitz, who took time out from her busy schedule to read and carefully comment on not only the chapter drafts but also the original proposal for the book. I am also indebted to Dennis Freeman, who shared his insights into the early years of Wickenburg's history with me, and to Ed Byerly, who drew the map that appears at the front of the book. The staff of the Wickenburg Public Library—in particular Rosemary Clark—was very helpful when I sought information on the town's history from the library's files, as were the pleasant and efficient staff members at the Luhrs Reading Room and Arizona Historical Foundation, both at Arizona State University's Hayden Library.

Finally, I want to thank the donors whose financial generosity has made this history of Wickenburg possible. Dallas "Rusty" Gant Jr. and Corinne Quayle provided the initial funding for the research and writing of the book; without their support and encouragement, the project might never have been undertaken. The museum also received support from the Arizona Humanities Council, which provided a grant to help defray research costs.

The Town on
the Hassayampa

1 Following the Water as Far as It Goes

THE HASSAYAMPA RIVER, like all watercourses in the desert, has attracted people for centuries. Lined in many places with towering cottonwood trees, and supporting occasional oases of dense riparian vegetation, the Hassayampa has offered desert residents not only water but soil in which to grow food, wood for cooking and other uses, and shelter for game and edible plants.

To the Yavapai, the most recent Indian group to live in the Wickenburg area, the river was known as the Haseyamo or Hasayamo, which roughly translates as "following the water as far as it goes." The Haseyamo was an unusual river even in the desert, where the presence of a streambed has never been a guarantee of flowing or even standing water. Except in times of heavy rains or snows in the nearby mountains, when torrents of muddy water might surge down the Haseyamo's broad and often sandy bed, the river's flow was intermittent even in the wettest of seasons.

Because bedrock was located deep below the riverbed in many places, the water flowing downstream often disappeared underground in the sandy river bottom soil, resurfacing periodically where the bedrock rose to the level of the riverbed. On many parts of the river, especially in the vicinity of present-day Wickenburg, standing pools of water might be the only evidence that the stream was a perennial one. In other stretches, such as the section now included in the Hassa-

3

yampa River Preserve, the surface flow might be vigorous through-out the year, creating a lush riparian environment that attracted birds, game, and other wildlife. Elsewhere, particularly for long stretches as it approached its junction with the Gila River, the riverbed was a dry expanse of soil and rock.

The Anglo Americans who began frequenting the region in the 1860s called the river the Hassayampa, approximating the Yavapai name. The first party of miners to ascend the river from its junction with the Gila at first found no evidence that the river was a perennial one. "We had to follow its dry, sandy bed quite a distance into the hills through a gorge-like channel before we reached the damp sand at a point to which the water had flown the day before," Daniel Conner later wrote. "It is quite common in this dry country for the water to gradually cease to flow at night and then extend its distance as the sun rises."

Although Conner did not find the region much to his liking—he called it "the roughest country to be composed of ordinary hills and mountains that I had yet seen in all my Rocky Mountain experi-ences"—the Hassayampa had long been important to the western branch of the Yavapai people. The western Yavapai's traditional home-land encompassed much of western Arizona, which has always been a land of scant food resources and few reliable water sources. The climate of the Hassayampa drainage was mild in the winter and, ow-ing to its moderate elevation of just over two thousand feet, not as severely hot in the summer as the desert expanse to the west. Although the Yavapai did not live year-round in the river valley, they built *ranche-rias,* or villages, up and down the valley, which they occupied season-ally while cultivating corn, pumpkins, and other crops in the rich valley soil.

Not far from the site of present-day Wickenburg—which the early Anglo pioneers dubbed the Pumpkin Patch—the river leaves a nar-row canyon and passes through a small basin rimmed with low hills. To the east rise the Bradshaw Mountains, whose pine-clad upper slopes are often snow-covered in the winter. The Hassayampa originates near the northern reaches of the Bradshaws, in a small mountain range called the Sierra Prieta. Fed by the streams draining the western slopes of the Bradshaws, as well as by a few watercourses flowing out of the drier mountains to the west, it flows southward through the Bradshaw foothills and past the Weaver Mountains before reaching the canyon, which is just north of the townsite.

Just south of the canyon, two intermittent creeks—Martinez Wash and Antelope Creek—join the river. At the townsite itself, another intermittent creek—Sols Wash—intersects the Hassayampa, though it rarely contributes water to the stream's flow. In addition to the Bradshaws, which dominate the eastern skyline, several small mountain ranges rise above the townsite—the Wickenburg, Buckhorn, and Hieroglyphic mountains to the east, and the Weaver and Date Creek mountains to the north. Far to the west lie the Harquahala and Harcuvar ranges, separated from Wickenburg by the level expanse of the Aguila Valley. To the south lie the Vulture Mountains, beyond which stretches the Hassayampa Plain, sloping imperceptibly south toward the Gila River.

The Yavapai Indians

While the river valley was fertile and its winter climate mild, it still could support only a limited population. Nevertheless, the Hassayampa valley was probably the most hospitable country frequented by the western branch of the Yavapai, whose traditional homeland was bordered on the south by the Gila River, the west by the Colorado River, the north by the Bill Williams and Santa Maria rivers, and the east by the crest of the Bradshaw Mountains. The broad expanse of desert that stretched westward from the Hassayampa was a harsh land, stingy with its resources, while cold and occasional snow rendered the mountain ranges in western and central Arizona livable only part of the year. Consequently, the Yavapai who frequented the Hassayampa River valley were never very numerous—perhaps as few as five hundred altogether.

The western Yavapai (or Tolkapaya, as they called themselves) were one of three branches of the Yavapai people. The others were the northeastern Yavapai (Yavepe, from which the name Yavapai was derived), who frequented the eastern slopes of the Bradshaws near the site of Prescott and the Verde Valley, and the southeastern Yavapai (Kewevkapaya), whose homeland took in the upper San Pedro River, the Superstition Mountains, the western slopes of the Mazatzal Mountains, and part of the lower Verde Valley. Altogether, the Yavapai people numbered no more than two thousand, and perhaps as few as fifteen hundred, in an area that encompassed more than twenty thousand square miles of land.

As the Spaniards, Mexicans, and Anglo Americans who later came to Arizona were to discover, the Indian groups living in the Southwest enjoyed complex and often acrimonious relations among themselves. Among the three branches or bands of the Yavapai, each seems to have occupied a clearly defined area but to have allowed the others access to certain food resources—game or acorns in the mountains, for example—on a seasonal basis. Furthermore, the Yavapai bands cooperated in waging warfare against some of their neighbors. Relations with the O'odham (Pimas) and Maricopas to the south, and the Walapai to the north, were especially tense; raiding parties from all sides frequently traveled great distances to attack the *rancherias,* fields, and hunting parties of their enemies. Consequently, the Yavapai were in a permanent state of belligerency with both their southern and northern neighbors.

The Yavapai were on reasonably good terms with the Mohaves and Quechans of the Colorado River valley, with whom they often traded. The Yavapai enjoyed a more complex relationship with the Apaches, whose extensive homeland lay east of Yavapai territory; contacts between these two peoples varied from intermarriage to occasional hostilities, which consisted primarily of raids by small parties of warriors. Because the Yavapai and Apaches shared many cultural traits, the former were often mistaken for the latter by Spaniards and, especially, by Anglo Americans—much to the eventual misfortune of the Yavapai.

The three subtribes or branches of the Yavapai—western, northeastern, and southeastern—were divided into bands made up of families, with anywhere from two to ten families joining together on a voluntary basis. Yavapai were generally monogamous—polygamy was relatively rare, as was divorce—with women marrying soon after puberty, and men waiting until their twenties so that they might first prove their skill as hunters. The composition of the bands was flexible, with members joining or leaving as they saw fit. For the most part, each band lived apart from the others (just as the three subtribes generally stayed in their own territories), but on occasion they might join together on war expeditions against other tribes. Bands joined these expeditions voluntarily and always remained under the nominal leadership of their own war chiefs, who had risen to prominence based on their distinguished records in battle and persuasive oratorical powers. Because most of the warfare in which the Yavapai were involved originated in localized conflicts between bands or individuals, it was not uncommon for a band to decline to join another in a military expedition. In warfare, as in other affairs, political authority among the Yavapai was diffuse and, in comparison to Hispanic and Anglo cultures, decentralized.

As hunters and gatherers, the Yavapai were often on the move. In the winter, they frequented the lower elevations in their territory; in the summer, they moved between the mountains and deserts depending on which wild foods were ready for harvesting at the time. In the fall, they gathered acorns and other nuts, as well as seeds and berries. In the spring, they foraged for wild greens, while their summers were spent harvesting wild fruits, especially cactus fruits such as the tasty buds of the saguaro. Agave, which was a staple food for the Yavapai, was harvested year-round; the Yavapai often stayed in an agave-harvesting area for several months at a time as they gathered the plants, baked them in fire pits, and dried the cooked pulp for future use. Also year-round, the men hunted for deer, coyote, fox, rabbits, and antelope. When these game animals were scarce, everyone joined in catching lizards and insects.

In addition to foraging for wild foods, the Yavapai also farmed. Planting their fields in washes, river beds (especially the Hassayampa), and near springs, they grew corn, beans, squash, pumpkins, and tobacco. After planting their fields, they often left—intertribal warfare sometimes made it dangerous to stay in one place too long—and returned periodically to weed and occasionally to water the plants, and finally to harvest in the fall.

The Yavapai were distinctive in their appearance, owing to long hair bangs worn by both men and women. Spanish explorers and missionaries were convinced that these bangs, which generally reached the eyebrows, were worn in the shape of a cross, and so they called the Yavapai "Cruzados," or people of the cross. Both men and women wore garments made of skins—breechcloths for the men (with leggings and ponchos added in wintertime), and skirts and shirts for the women. In addition, they often painted their bodies with red clay as protection against the sun's rays. Some Yavapai women tattooed their faces, but for the most part, ornamentation was confined to bead necklaces and bracelets, as well as nose and ear rings, which both men and women wore.

Although they relied to a great extent on wild foods and game for their survival, the Yavapai were not entirely nomadic. Each band had camps, or *rancherias,* to which it would return each year according to a fairly regular pattern. These might be caves and rock shelters, in which fires could be built, for winter use, or huts of grass thatch and wood poles covered with mud and skins for summer use. In addition, they employed *ramadas*—simple shade shelters built of cottonwood poles and grass thatch—to protect themselves from the intense summer sun.

Spanish Exploration in Central Arizona

The most significant contacts that the Yavapai had with other peoples were intertribal in nature: warfare with the Walapai, Pimas, and Maricopas, and generally peaceful relations with the Apaches, Navajos, Hopis, and Colorado River tribes. Although the Spaniards mounted periodic *entradas,* or exploratory expeditions, into what would later be called Arizona, they had only the briefest of encounters with the Yavapai. Indeed, Spanish contacts with the Yavapai were so few, and the records they left of those contacts so sketchy, that most of what we know about the Yavapai's traditional culture and territory is based on interviews and observations made after the tribe had been defeated by the Anglo Americans and confined to reservations.

The first Spaniard to enter the Yavapai's territory was Antonio de Espejo, a *conquistador* who entered the Verde Valley from the east in 1582–83 and appears to have traveled as far west as the Bill Williams River—a journey that took him through the northeastern Yavapai's territory and across the northern edge of the western Yavapai's territory. Espejo's original mission had been to rescue several Franciscan missionaries left alone in New Mexico. Upon arrival in New Mexico, however, he learned that the missionaries had died, so instead he set out to explore the surrounding territory, eventually ending up in Arizona. Somewhere in western Arizona—perhaps in the Verde Valley—Espejo claimed to have discovered several potentially rich mines.

After Espejo returned to New Spain (Mexico) and reported his findings, Spain's interest in Arizona quickened, though little was done about it for some time. In 1598, the second Spaniard to visit the Yavapai, Marcos Farfán de los Godos, arrived in the Verde Valley. He had been sent by Don Juan de Oñate, a wealthy man who helped discover the silver mines of Zacatecas and had been authorized by the viceroy of New Spain to conquer and settle Spain's northern frontier in present-day Arizona and New Mexico. Specifically, Farfán was looking for the mines reportedly seen by Espejo. He, too, journeyed as far as the Bill Williams River before returning to New Mexico, where he had left Oñate. According to Farfán, he met the Yavapai Indians—probably both western and northeastern—and gave them the name Cruzados, after the crosses he said they displayed on their foreheads.

Six years later, in 1604, Don Juan de Oñate himself retraced Farfán's steps, on an ambitious expedition to the Pacific coast conceived as a last-ditch attempt to save his New Mexico colony, which had been a financial disappointment to the *conquistador*. Oñate hoped to find not only the mines reported by Espejo and Farfán, but also additional ones, thus making his colonizing venture more remunerative.

Unfortunately for Oñate and for Spain, he found none of the mineral wealth he was seeking. He did, though, make contact with most of the Indian tribes that occupied northern and western Arizona, as well as the lower California desert. His travels in western Arizona took him through the Verde Valley, across the mountains to the Big Sandy River, then down that river and the Bill Williams River to the Colorado River, which he followed southward to the ford at the site of present-day Yuma. About the Yavapai Indians, whom he met, Oñate later reported to the viceroy: "They call these Indians Cruzados on account of some crosses which all, little and big, suspend from the lock of hair that falls over the forehead." He explained the peculiar adornment as the result of an earlier encounter that the Indians supposedly had with white missionaries. Whether these actually were crosses, or the product of Oñate's wishful thinking, remains a mystery.

After Oñate, the Yavapai and other inland tribes in western Arizona saw no more of the Spanish until 1776, when a Franciscan monk, Francisco Garcés, traveled through Yavapai territory en route to the Hopi pueblos from the lower Colorado River. Garcés was the first Spaniard to call the Indians by their own name, identifying them as Yavipai, after Yavepe, the tribal name used by the northeastern Yavapai. However, he also was the last Spaniard to visit any part of Yavapai territory; for the rest of the Spanish period in the Southwest, the Yavapai and other inland tribes of western Arizona remained entirely beyond the reach of the Spanish empire. When they were noticed at all, the Yavapai generally were referred to as "mountain people" or "wanderers" and often confused with the Apaches.

At no time during these early explorations by Spanish *conquistadores* and missionaries does it appear that any Spaniard entered the Hassayampa River valley. In most of their travels across western Arizona, they stayed close to the Gila River and had no reason to venture northward. Whatever contact the western Yavapai had with the Spanish was likely indirect—conversations with northeastern Yavapai who had seen Spaniards—or occurred outside their usual territory, perhaps when western Yavapai ventured into Quechan territory and visited the Franciscan mission that was briefly established on the lower Colorado River from 1779 to 1781.

The Fur Trappers

Following Garces' brief visit to the Yavapai homeland, Spanish interest in the northernmost reaches of its American empire declined; beset by internal bureaucratic problems and distracted by conflict with other European nations, imperial officials chose to forego expansion in the interest of protecting Spain's existing holdings in the Americas. When colonial rebellion led to Mexico's declaration of independence in 1821, the Spanish presence in Arizona consisted of only a handful of settlements in the Santa Cruz River valley. Although the new Mexican government tried to encourage settlement in Arizona, its efforts were largely unsuccessful and much of the territory was abandoned to its native inhabitants.

For the next two decades, the only non-Indians to penetrate the interior of Arizona were fur trappers and traders operating out of Taos and Santa Fe. Yet even they generally avoided western Arizona, and there is no evidence that any of the trappers reached the Hassayampa River valley, for the Hassayampa lacked beaver, whose pelts were the object of the Southwestern fur trade during its brief existence in the 1820s and 1830s. In contrast, the Gila River watershed had a large beaver population, which meant that most of the trappers' travels were confined to the Gila River valley and to tributary streams such as the Salt and Verde rivers.

The closest any of the mountain men appears to have come to the Hassayampa region was in 1829, when a party led by Ewing Young traveled up the Verde River from the Salt River and then split into two groups, one of which headed west. This party, led by Kit Carson, stayed well north of the Bill Williams River en route to the Colorado River and to California, their ultimate destination. Even though the trappers appear to have stayed away from Yavapai territory, they still had contact with the tribe. Several bloody encounters between the fur trappers and Yavapai warriors are believed to have occurred, most notably a battle between Young's party and southeastern Yavapai on the Salt River in 1829. Some historians think that Young initiated this encounter in retaliation for an earlier attack, in 1826, in which the southeastern Yavapai nearly wiped out a trapping expedition led by Miguel Robidoux.

Early United States Exploration

After the brief forays of the fur trappers, Anglo Americans for the most part stayed away from Arizona. However, when the United States went to war with Mexico in 1846, Americans once again directed their attention to Arizona and New Mexico as the war quickly evolved into a contest over resource-rich California. With the principal southern land routes to California lying across Mexico's northern frontier—now the American Southwest—it became imperative for the United States government to gain control of the region.

In all, three columns of United States troops traversed Arizona during the brief war: one under Brig. Gen. Stephen Watts Kearney, a second (the Mormon Battalion) commanded by Col. Philip St. George Cooke, and a third under the command of Maj. Lawrence P. Graham. However, none of them went farther north than the Gila River, which by now was established as the main "highway" across Arizona. Most argonauts (California gold-seekers) and other travelers to California, who called this route the Gila Trail, stayed on the river and had no reason to enter the Hassayampa River drainage. It is possible, but unlikely, that the columns of American soldiers had some contact with Yavapai Indians along the Gila River, for the Yavapai generally were reluctant to venture so close to the territory of their bitter enemies, the Pimas and Maricopas.

When the federal government began sending survey parties into the Southwest to look for prospective railroad and wagon routes, the Hassayampa region again escaped scrutiny, for it lay in a large band of mountainous territory in central Arizona that did not seem well-suited to development as a transportation corridor. Two railroad surveys of southern Arizona—one conducted in 1854 by A. B. Gray for the Texas Western Railroad, the other in 1854–55 by Lt. John G. Parke for the Army Corps of Topographical Engineers—examined much of the route eventually followed by the Southern Pacific, which went no farther north than the Gila River. Likewise, two northern surveys by the Army never approached the Hassayampa watershed. In 1851, Capt. Lorenzo Sitgreaves took a surveying party across northern Arizona, passing just below the Grand Canyon. Two years later, Lt. Amiel W. Whipple led an expedition that examined a possible railroad route along the 35th parallel. He followed Sitgreaves' path through eastern Arizona but then left it to travel down the Big Sandy and Bill Williams rivers to the Colorado—a route that took him along the edge of, but not into, western Yavapai territory.

The limited encounters between Anglo Americans and the Yavapai portended changes far greater than the small number of persons involved might suggest. If the Anglo Americans continued to show an interest in the area, their penetration of the Yavapai homeland might well produce more bloodshed and almost certainly would bring changes for the native inhabitants. Although the Yavapai had so far managed to survive three-and-a-half centuries of contact with Spaniards and Anglo Americans without any significant impact on their culture and subsistence economy, the army and railroad surveys were indications that their isolation was about to end.

2 The Vulture Mine and the Founding of Wickenburg

ALTHOUGH ANGLO AMERICANS had been passing through Arizona for nearly four decades since their arrival in the mid-1820s, they had shown scant interest in the territory itself. Concerned primarily with crossing Arizona, rather than occupying it, American soldiers, surveyors, and gold-seekers generally kept close to the Gila River, only occasionally venturing away from the river valley to explore other parts of the territory, primarily its northern reaches. Most importantly, they only barely penetrated the vast region of western and central Arizona occupied by the Yavapai Indians. Now, however, two parties of gold-seeking prospectors, working in the same area but without any knowledge of each other, were about to direct attention to the mineral-rich mountains of central Arizona, in the heart of the territory occupied by the western and northeastern Yavapai. Should their efforts yield any substantial claims, more miners were certain to follow. When that happened, the isolation that had so far protected the Yavapai would be breached permanently, with momentous consequences for the tribe.

Early Gold Discoveries

The mining boom in western Arizona began in earnest in 1862, when Pauline Weaver and other adventurers discovered gold placers along the Colorado River north of Fort Yuma. Almost overnight the town of La Paz sprung up on the river's eastern bank; by the end of the year, at least fifteen hundred people were living in tents and adobe dwellings in the settlement, which quickly became a beehive of mining and commercial activity. Some of these prospectors were men from the California gold fields who, having failed to make their fortunes there, now sought new opportunities in the interior regions of the West. A significant number were Mexicans from Arizona and Sonora, many of whom brought their families, as well as traditional skills and technology well adapted to the special requirements of desert mining. However, the placers proved to be short-lived. In less than a year, miners were leaving La Paz to search for gold in other locations, among them the Hassayampa River and Bradshaw Mountains.

The first such party to leave La Paz for the interior of Arizona was organized by Abraham Peeples and left in the spring of 1863, with Pauline Weaver as its guide. After traveling north along the Colorado to the Bill Williams River, the Peeples party turned eastward. They followed the river to its upper reaches and then struck out cross-country, eventually arriving at a small mountain they dubbed Antelope Peak, located in the Weaver Mountains about fifteen miles north of the eventual site of Wickenburg. Here they made several gold discoveries, the most famous of which was Rich Hill, an unusual placer deposit located not in a wash or river valley, as was typical, but atop the hill itself.

Accounts of the Rich Hill discovery vary, but it seems clear it was accidental; according to one popular version, the placers were located by two Mexican miners who happened to cross the hill while prospecting the surrounding countryside. (Although they were not members of the Peeples party, the two men very generously agreed to let the others share in their discovery.) At first, the men pried gold nuggets from crevices and rocks with their knives. After these easy pickings had been exhausted, though, they were forced to use more conventional and time-consuming methods of mining, such as sluicing and panning gravel taken from the hill and nearby creekbeds. When water was not available—which was often—they employed dry-washing, a dusty and laborious process similar to winnowing chaff from grain; in its simplest form, dry-washing was done by throwing the gravel into the air and letting the wind take away the lighter rocks and dirt.

Peeples, Weaver, and their companions no doubt thought they were the first gold miners to enter the Hassayampa region, but in fact Joseph Walker and his men had been exploring the mountains above the river valley for several weeks. Walker's party, which came to the area not from La Paz but from the east, had ascended the Hassayampa River in the winter of 1863 and started prospecting in the Bradshaw Mountains that spring. He and his men established a permanent camp just south of the eventual site of Prescott and then made several placer discoveries in the vicinity of Mt. Union, along the upper Hassayampa near its headwaters. After forming the Pioneer Mining District and registering their early claims, Walker's men cached their supplies and headed south toward the Pima Indian villages, where they hoped to obtain supplies before returning to develop their claims. There they met Weaver and several others from the Peeples party who also had come to buy food from the Pimas.

Word of the gold discoveries spread among the few Anglos and Mexicans who lived in the vicinity of the Gila River, and they in turn helped carry the news to the outside world. Soon miners began to enter the Hassayampa region in significant numbers. Other gold strikes in the Bradshaws soon followed, among them finds at Lynx Creek, Granite Creek, Big Bug, and Groom Creek. By the end of the summer, the Walker Mining District had been organized and the town of Walker had begun to take shape near the Lynx Creek diggings. At the same time, activity was picking up farther south on the Hassayampa, near Rich Hill. In addition to the unusual hilltop find, Mexican and Anglo miners discovered modest amounts of gold in nearby Antelope and Weaver creeks. They organized the Weaver Mining District in May 1864, and a settlement named after Pauline Weaver soon became the center of activity in that district. By the end of the summer, Weaver had a population of more than a thousand persons— some estimates range as high as fifteen hundred—most of whom were

Mexican miners from Sonora, southern Arizona, La Paz, and other Colorado River diggings.

Intrigued by the gold discoveries along the Hassayampa, Brig. Gen. James H. Carleton, the Union commander of the Department of New Mexico—which included Arizona—sent New Mexico's surveyor general, John Clark, to inspect the area. Reporting to Carleton in September 1863, Clark was cautiously optimistic. "From my own observation and from statements of those in whom I believe I can rely, I am satisfied that there is gold in paying quantities in all the streams prospected in the entire district," he wrote. However, Clark also told Carleton that the Hassayampa lacked a reliable supply of water and good timber, and he was uncertain about the agricultural potential of the valley. In fact, his report made it clear that the prospects for the Hassayampa region, although good, were not spectacular. "Labor— hard and continued labor—is required in this new field to procure gold in amounts to compensate men for going there," he observed. "The chances are that they will make no more than ordinary wages, if industrious."

Like other observers before and after him, Clark noted the predominance in the Weaver district of Mexican miners. "I was sorry to learn," he told Carleton, "that there was much ill-feeling between them and our citizens, and fear they may have serious trouble, unless there should be a military force stationed there at an early day to preserve order." Almost from the moment they began arriving in the area, the Mexican miners were not well received by the Anglos who also were arriving in ever-larger numbers. Using the articles and bylaws of the two mining districts as their weapons, Anglos in the Walker and Weaver districts moved quickly to restrict the rights of Mexicans and, where possible, bar them from working their own claims. Both districts refused to allow Mexicans to stake any claims during the first six months' of the districts' existence, and later the districts adopted rules that restricted the hiring of Mexican miners. Of the two districts, the Walker was the more hostile toward Mexican miners. Its bylaws at first required Anglos to pay a fee for every Mexican they hired and then banned the employment of Mexicans altogether. Tensions increased to the point where, at about the time Clark visited, armed Anglo miners forcibly evicted a group of Mexicans from their claims along the upper Hassayampa River.

It is not surprising that such hostility was shown toward Mexicans in the Walker district, for it was there that the more lucrative claims had been found. Its placers were more productive than those in the Weaver district, and it showed more promise as a lode mining district as well. In contrast, the placers in the Weaver district were already beginning to be exhausted. Gradually Walker became a predominantly Anglo town, and Weaver a predominantly Mexican community. When central Arizona's first military post, Fort Whipple, was established in December 1863 in response to pleas by the miners for protection from the Yavapai, it was located about twenty miles north of present-day Prescott, leaving Weaver vulnerable to Indian attacks. By the summer of 1864, Weaver was in rapid decline and its population dwindling as many of its residents moved to the new town of Wickenburg. Walker also lost population to another new town, Prescott, which was founded in May 1864 near the relocated site of Fort Whipple, recently moved to the banks of Granite Creek from its original location in the Chino Valley.

Discovery of the Vulture Mine

Exactly when Henry Wickenburg first arrived in the Hassayampa area is a matter of dispute. Some say he came with the Peeples party and was present for the discovery of Rich Hill, others that he came after the first rush to the Weaver placers. A German immigrant, Wickenburg was born in Essen, Prussia, in 1819 and left Europe in 1847 to come to the United States. No one knows exactly what he did after his arrival here, except that he spent some time in California before coming to Arizona in either 1861 or 1862. After a brief stint at Fort Yuma and then at La Paz, where he tried his hand at placer mining, Wickenburg moved on to central Arizona; he eventually settled in Peeples Valley, where he was living in 1863, the year he undertook his most famous prospecting trip.

Hearing of gold prospects in the Harquahala Mountains, Wickenburg set out from his ranch with two other men, E. A. Van Bibber and Theodore Green Rusk, on a trip to the mountains. On their way back from the Harquahalas, where they failed to discover anything of particular interest, Wickenburg became interested in a prominent white quartz ledge that protruded from a ridge of low mountains just west of the Hassayampa River. His companions did not share his enthusiasm for the location, however, and the three men returned to their homes without filing a claim.

Wickenburg, though, remained convinced that the ledge offered promise as a gold mine location. Within the month, he returned to the site alone, this time finding rock samples that bore evidence of gold. When he showed the samples to his two erstwhile companions, they agreed to return to the site for another inspection. This time they were impressed, and together they filed a location notice for the mine claim, which they called the Vulture.

Exactly how that name was applied to the mine, and to the mountains at whose base it was located, is shrouded in legend. According to one version, Wickenburg had seen a vulture perched nearby while he was prospecting the area; according to another, he shot and killed a vulture perched on the quartz ledge, and then discovered the valuable ore samples when he went to inspect his prey. One newspaper man, writing in the *Arizona Republican* in 1897, took note of the conflicting stories and attributed them to "Eastern papers" that felt compelled to invent a fanciful tale of the mine's discovery. According to him, Wickenburg's own story was more prosaic. "I always liked short names," George Smalley quoted the elderly miner as saying, "and it just came into my head to call it the Vulture. The rock was very dark, and it did not look much like quartz." Whether this is the "true" version is impossible to verify; Wickenburg appears to have related several versions of the story himself—or, at least, his listeners seem to have heard what they wanted.

At any rate, neither Wickenburg nor his companions did anything to develop the mine at first, despite their initial enthusiasm about the claim. Van Bibber and Rusk actually left the area, leaving Wickenburg alone and living in very modest circumstances on the banks of the Hassayampa River several miles from the claim site. Eventually even Wickenburg left, returning in May 1864 to find the site deserted and showing no evidence that anyone had tried to work the claim. He filed a second claim with four new partners, and together they organized the Wickenburg Mining District, registered their claim at Prescott, and started development work on the mine. After digging out a ton of ore, which they laboriously hauled to the Hassayampa River, Wickenburg and his partners built an *arrastra*, or stone ore-grinding tub, and began processing the rock. Their labors yielded a promising amount of gold, although like everything else having to do with the Vulture Mine, exactly how much is disputed. Figures as high as $305 appear in some accounts, while Charles Genung, who claimed to have helped Wickenburg build his first *arrastra*, asserted in his memoirs that only about a hundred dollars in gold was taken out.

Even at the lower figure, it was a substantial sum of money, enough to encourage Wickenburg and the others to continue their development work—and enough for Rusk and two other men to file a lawsuit against Wickenburg alleging that they were being cheated out of Rusk's one-third interest in the mine. The suit, which was the first piece of mining litigation heard in Arizona's territorial courts, argued that the original claim filed by Van Bibber, Rusk, and Wickenburg was still valid, and that Rusk's sale of his interest to the two men gave them part ownership of the Vulture Mine. Fortunately for Wickenburg, the plaintiffs lost on the grounds that he and his two original companions had never properly registered their claim at the territorial capital.

Free of any cloud over his ownership of the mine, Wickenburg set about promoting the Vulture's full development. Rather than work the mine himself, Wickenburg let others take out ore in return for a payment of $15 per ton. By late fall, operations at the mine and on the banks of the Hassayampa were in full swing, with various groups of miners taking out as much as seven hundred dollars in gold each day. By 1865, about forty *arrastras* were in use along the riverbank. The *arrastra* process, which was first developed by Spanish miners, required no machinery and thus was well adapted to the conditions that prevailed at the Vulture, whose isolation made the importation of processing equipment an expensive and time-consuming undertaking. The partially crushed ore was placed in a large stone tub, along with water and mercury (quicksilver), and the mixture slowly ground into a slurry by large rocks suspended from a wooden pole turned by horses or mules. Eventually the gold amalgamated, or combined, with the mercury. When the resulting amalgam was heated in a retort or oven, the mercury ran off, leaving a clump of gold.

As word of the mine and its development spread across the country, it attracted not only miners but also journalists. One correspondent, writing for the *Hartford Evening Press* in Connecticut, predicted that "a stream of gold will pour from the Hassayampa when the quartz mills arrive, and all this tedious process is done by the power of steam. There is no portion of the mineral region so favorable for the working of a large mine." To a large extent, his prophecy was realized. Toward the end of the summer of 1865, a small stamp mill was erected at the intersection of Martinez Wash and the Hassayampa River—on the opposite side of the river bottom from the present-day Remuda Ranch—giving the miners an easier and more efficient mechanism for reducing, or crushing, the ore prior to amalgamation.

With ore valued as high as $80 per ton, the Vulture Mine was bound to attract the attention of investors. In late 1865, Wickenburg, who had acquired sole ownership of the Vulture claim by this time, sold his interest in the mine to a group of New York men led by Behtchuel Phelps. After paying Wickenburg $25,000 for several hundred feet of the Vulture lode—the most valuable part of the claim—as well as the stamp mill, which Wickenburg had recently taken over, the buyers incorporated the Vulture Mining Company and began placing orders for new ore processing machinery.

The Founding of Wickenburg

Located as it was away from the Hassayampa River, the mine site itself could not support more than a limited number of miners and their families. Consequently, the main settlement that grew up in association with the Vulture Mine took shape along the river, which at its closest passed ten miles east of the mine site. Here, where the Yavapai had raised pumpkins and established a series of *rancherias*, the miners found an abundance of wood and water, which they used not only for domestic uses but, more importantly, to run their *arrastras* and amalgamation ovens.

At first, miners simply camped out near their own *arrastras*, so that the unnamed settlement consisted of nothing more than a string of tent camps scattered along the river over a five-mile stretch. Soon, though, activity began to concentrate near the stamp mill at Martinez Wash and the Hassayampa River. Not far south, Henry Wickenburg had established his home along the Hassayampa River, and gradually other residences and a handful of businesses congregated nearby. How the settlement acquired the name of Wickenburg is unclear, but it appears that a guest at Wickenburg's place, James Moore, used the name "Wickenburg Ranch" as the return address on several letters he wrote to Arizona's territorial governor while staying at the settlement in 1864. Eventually, the name was shortened to Wickenburg.

Like many other mining towns, Wickenburg grew in a haphazard manner. At first, it was little more than a camp, as described in November 1864 by the *Hartford Evening Press* correspondent: "It was a busy scene. Two arrastias [sic] were at work on my left, a half dozen men were breaking rock small enough for the arrastias, a steer was being butchered under a tree, midway the cook was busy over a huge fire, a long mess table under the trees near by, to the right were piles of flour and wheat in sacks, huge loaded wagons, a dozen horses feeding, and the same little tent of last spring [in which Henry Wickenburg once lived]."

Soon the tents were replaced by adobe dwellings. In June 1865, while the town was still just a collection of scattered houses, a post office was established. Two years later, Gen. James E. Rusling passed through Wickenburg while on an inspection tour for the War Department. He found a small town with about two hundred inhabitants, composed of simple adobe buildings and dependent on the working of the Vulture Mine for its livelihood. In fact, Rusling had little to say about the town itself, choosing instead to describe the mine and related structures such as the new twenty-stamp mill, which the company had recently installed along Martinez Wash in a "fine adobe structure."

It was not until a year later, in 1868, that a townsite was platted by Wickenburg and surveyed by Robert Groom, who earlier had laid out the town of Prescott. (As it turned out, this plat was never officially recorded, and Wickenburg had to resurvey the town at the turn of the century.) One problem that promoters faced was the Hassayampa valley's reputation as a sickly place, owing to malaria, which was common along many Arizona rivers. In 1867, several town dwellers died of the disease. Two years later, the editor of Prescott's *Weekly Arizona Miner* described Wickenburg as "unhealthy" and wondered why the standing water in its vicinity had not yet been drained. With such improvements, John Marion advised, the town would prosper. "We see no good reason, except that of sickness," Marion observed, "why Wickenburg should not grow to be the size of Virginia City, Nevada, inside of the next five years."

Apparently, the incidence of malaria declined over the next few years; as with other Arizona rivers, it is likely that development, cattle grazing, and increased water consumption by miners and town dwellers all contributed to a reduction in the amount of standing water in which malaria-bearing mosquitoes could breed in the Hassayampa riverbed. Slowly the population of the town increased. When a census-taker arrived in 1870, he found 442 persons (74 of them women) living in Wickenburg and its immediate vicinity, which included the Vulture Mine and Vulture City, located fifteen miles away from the town.

All reports from the time indicate a substantial, perhaps even a majority, Hispanic presence in Wickenburg. The *placeros,* or gold placer miners from Mexico and Arizona, had left Weaver after its placers began to run out and gradually migrated south to Wickenburg and the Vulture Mine. When Rusling visited in 1867, he found that more than half the men working at the Vulture were Mexican. In fact,

Mexicans and Mexican Americans appear to have been the major labor source in Wickenburg, working as woodcutters, charcoal burners, packers, and freighters, and providing valuable expertise in the operation of the *arrastras*. In addition, they were prominent among the farmers and ranchers who took up land in the Hassayampa valley.

A year after the census-taker had visited, D. S. Chamberlain arrived in the new town and, with a partner, bought a blacksmith shop. "We made money right from the start," he recalled years later in a newspaper article. "The Vulture mine and mill were running full blast. Ten mule teams would go to the mill every day, load up with ore and 10 loaded teams would leave the mine daily for the mill. The company paid off every other Tuesday. Money was plentiful, wages high and all seemed to be good spenders." According to Chamberlain, the town was home to five saloons and one restaurant. The main gathering place for miners and businessmen was the Magnolia, a brewery and saloon owned by Abraham H. Peeples, who had organized the gold-seeking party that discovered the Weaver placers. A weekly line of stages connected Wickenburg with Prescott, Tucson, Phoenix, and California. "The town was full of prospectors, coming and going, and frequently squads of soldiers," Chamberlain recalled.

Initial Development of the Vulture Mine

As Chamberlain's account makes clear, the newly formed Vulture Mining Company invested substantial sums of money in the Vulture. In 1866, less than a year after purchasing the mine from Wickenburg, the company sunk a new inclined shaft and set up a new twenty-stamp mill and amalgamation facility, which was located not at the mine but on the town's outskirts, at the intersection of Martinez Wash and the Hassayampa. Within a year, however, the company had overextended itself financially in a battle against high operating costs and was taken over by its creditors, who temporarily suspended mining operations. The problem, as outlined by Rusling in 1867, was simple: "Unfortunately, no water could be found near the mine, and all used there then was transported from Wickenburg, at a cost of ten cents per gallon. So, all the ore taken out had to be wagoned, from the mine to the mill at Wickenburg, at a cost of ten dollars per ton. The cost of everything else was about in the same proportion."

Fortunately for the town, the directors of the Vulture Mining Company were able to arrange their debts and resume control of the company. In 1867, the company took $146,000 in gold bullion from the mine; in 1868, $254,000. By 1870, the Vulture Mine accounted for half of the territory's gold production. More importantly, it employed as many as 150 men at a time, paying them wages as high as $70 per week. Near its stamp mill on Martinez Wash, the company put in a garden and built a boarding house, office, warehouse, and other structures. Sometimes referred to as the town of Vulture, this substantial cluster of buildings along the river was evidence that the Vulture Mining Company was more than Wickenburg's most substantial business; it was the town's economic lifeblood.

With the Vulture Mine apparently producing a steady stream of bullion, the fledgling community of Wickenburg had every reason to be optimistic about its prospects. However, the mine's high operating costs still cast a cloud over its future. As long as the ore body was rich and easily accessible, the costs could be absorbed. Should the ore decline in quality, the mine's owners might find it difficult to continue operations—as they had once before. In addition, mining operations throughout the region were hampered by guerrilla warfare with the Yavapai Indians, who had begun to strike at the miners, settlers, and ranchers coming into their homeland. As the residents of Wickenburg would soon discover, the fortunes of a frontier gold mining town were indeed precarious.

Yavapai women in front of their brush-and-blanket wickiup,
circa 1890.

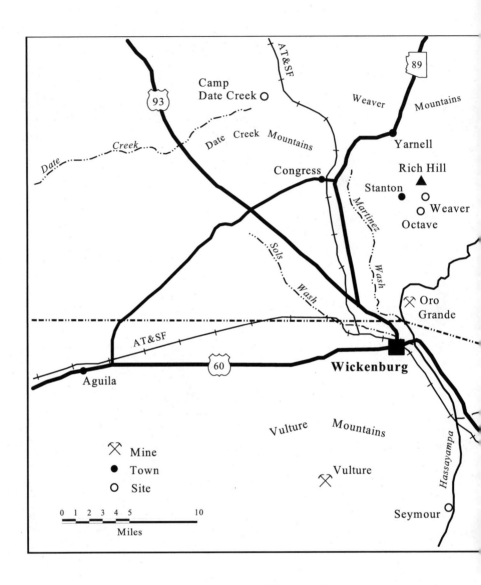

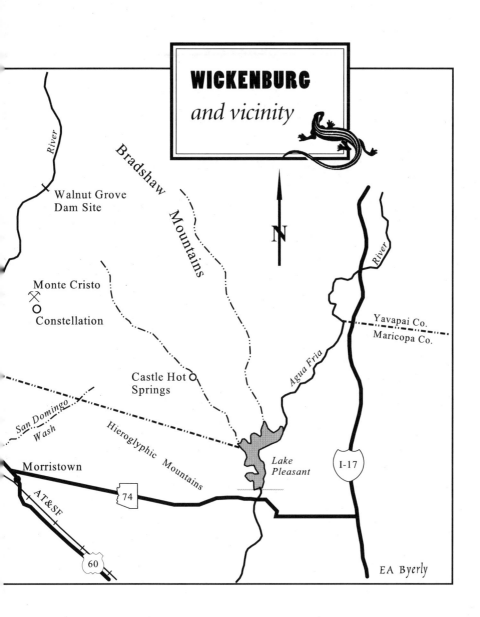

WICKENBURG
and vicinity

River

Bradshaw Mountains

Walnut Grove
Dam Site

N

Monte Cristo

Constellation

Castle Hot
Springs

San Domingo
Wash

Hieroglyphic Mountains

Agua Fria

River

Yavapai Co.
Maricopa Co.

Morristown

AT&SF

74

60

Lake
Pleasant

I-17

EA Byerly

Water wagon belonging to José Ocampo, departing for the Vulture Mine from Front Street near the Hassayampa River, circa 1912.

(Opposite) Cyanide plant at the Vulture Mine, sometime in the 1890s.

(Right) Wagons similar to this one carried ore from the Vulture Mine to the stamp mills near the Hassayampa River.

Mill at the Vulture Mine, circa 1900.

Henry Wickenburg.

Ygnacio Garcia.

The lake behind Walnut Grove Dam as it appeared in
the late 1880s, not long after the dam was built.

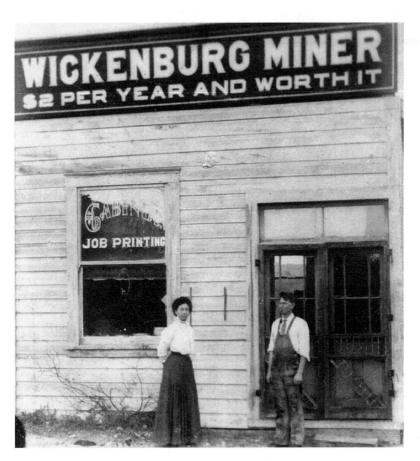

Angela Hammer, at left, was the owner and editor of
the Wickenburg *Miner*, which was published locally
beginning in 1904.

A group of local musicians, circa 1909, photographed after playing at a Wickenburg saloon. Those pictured are (from left to right) Chono Saavedra, Frank Bustamonte, unidentified, Eraclio Fimbres, John Charles Young, Frank Verdugo, unidentified, Manuel Ruiz, and Pedro Garcia.

José F. Quesada, a local rancher, circa 1911.

Henry Cowell, at right, was Wickenburg's first mayor. In this picture, taken around 1910, he was joined by John Riggs (second from right), Johnson Born (fourth from right), Jimmy Dunn (fifth from right), Ray Currie (second from left), and three other men.

The Ups and Downs
of a Gold Mining Town

3

ALTHOUGH BY THE EARLY 1870S the developers of the
Vulture Mine appeared to have overcome the difficulties posed by
the mine's remote location and distance from a reliable supply of water,
the struggle to keep the mine operating on a paying basis was just
beginning. As Wickenburg residents were to discover over the next
few decades, their fortunes were yoked to the Vulture Mine; the story
of Wickenburg's early years was, in many respects, one of continual
adaptation to the ups and downs of Arizona's most famous gold mine.
When it was productive, the Vulture brought wealth, settlers, and
business activity to Wickenburg. In bad times, when the vein disappeared or poor management led to a shutdown, the mine dragged
the economy of Wickenburg down with it. Deprived of wages, miners drifted away from the Hassayampa Valley, while business owners
struggled to stay afloat in hopes that new mineral discoveries would
bring back their customers.

In the meantime, though, the Anglo and Hispanic miners who came
to Wickenburg in the late 1860s confronted a more immediate problem, one they considered to be the greatest obstacle to the region's
settlement and development: warfare with the Yavapai Indians. Writing to the *Arizona Miner* in 1868, less than five years after the discovery of the Vulture, one Wickenburg resident lamented, "The Indians
can come here at night and kill us. We cannot watch them, at night, as

every man works during the day and needs rest at night. Now, Government should do something for us. Cannot the military commander at Fort Whipple spare us 20 men?"

Warfare with the Yavapai Indians

As the number of miners and settlers in the Bradshaw Mountains and Hassayampa River watershed increased, it was almost inevitable that conflict with the Yavapai would occur. For the Yavapai, the region's scarcity of resources had always made survival difficult; now they were forced to compete with the encroaching miners for game and water. The problem was especially acute along the river and at local springs. Anglo and Hispanic settlers often blocked access to water sources by filing water-right and homestead claims, and their thirsty livestock crowded around water holes and trampled valuable riparian vegetation. Also, as the Yavapai continued their seasonal migrations to hunt and gather wild foods, they found access to their traditional *rancherias* and agave-gathering sites impeded by settler and mining claims.

Much like the Apaches had done before, the Yavapai at first were guarded in their relations with the newcomers; they kept their distance for the most part, neither friendly nor especially hostile, waiting to see what impact the influx of strangers would have. Some miners were able to coexist for a time with the Yavapai; Pauline Weaver, for example, occasionally served as a mediator between the Yavapai and neighboring tribes, and he appears to have gone to some length to avoid conflict with the Indians he met while traveling and prospecting.

Most miners and settlers, though, saw the Yavapai as an enemy to be fought, killed, and driven off the land. It did not help matters that most whites considered the Yavapai to be Apaches, an association that automatically inclined the newcomers to regard the local Indians as enemies. As Charles Poston, the territory's first Indian agent, observed, the Yavapai were "not bad Indians, [but] occupy such an equivocal position that they are in constant danger of slaughter from the miners and frontiersmen." Even before the gold rush in the region, raids and killings were commonplace. In 1860, John "Jack" Swilling, an adventurer and promoter who later played an important role in the founding of Phoenix, led a party of Anglos and Maricopa Indians north from the Gila River to attack the Hassayampa *rancherias*, where they killed at least thirteen Yavapai and took several more as prisoners.

After the first mining rush, miners often formed parties that struck out from the camps to hunt down Indians, including women and children, and burn their *rancherias*. When two Yavapai boys wandered into the mining camp at Weaver during the winter of 1863–64 and were gunned down after being accused of theft by the miners, the Yavapai abandoned their watchful stance and struck back with attacks of their own. Soon the region was plunged into a violent cycle of raid and counter-raid, with no quarter given by either side. One Yavapai interviewed by soldiers at Fort Yuma in 1864, Qua-sha-ko-mah, complained that whites "had come into his country and taken some [of] their best planting places and told his people not to plant there any[more]. So many people in the Country had driven the game out, and made it scarce but if the Whites shot down his people the Indian law was blood for blood." The warfare, which continued for nine years, was intermittent and often vengeful in nature. No one knows exactly how many people were killed, but anthropologists estimate that between seven hundred and a thousand Yavapai lost their lives in the conflict, compared to about four hundred Anglos and Mexicans killed.

Typical of the conflict was a punitive expedition organized in January 1864 by Abraham Peeples and King Woolsey, two of several ranchers in the Hassayampa and Agua Fria river valleys who lost cattle and horses to raiding Indians they believed were Apaches but almost certainly were southeastern Yavapai. Striking out at the head of a group that included Anglos, Mexican Americans, Pimas, and Maricopas, Woolsey overtook his quarry near the junction of the Salt and Verde rivers. There he arranged a conference with the Indians, who enjoyed a marked superiority of numbers. At a prearranged signal, Woolsey's men opened fire on the unsuspecting Yavapai conferees, who lost at least nineteen men in the fusillade. In the ensuing confusion, Woolsey's party was able to escape with only one casualty, whom they buried in an improvised grave on the Salt River. When the men returned to their homes, they were welcomed as heroes. Woolsey in particular was commended by Arizona's legislature, which made him a colonel in the territorial militia that was being formed to combat the "Indian problem."

Despite such tactics, the Yavapai had the upper hand in the conflict during most of the 1860s. Moving freely throughout the countryside, which they knew intimately, they kept miners and settlers confined to the towns and camps. Writing to a California newspaper in 1865, a Wickenburg resident reported, "No man feels safe half a mile out from the settlements. 23 of my own personal acquaintances have been killed, stripped and mangled by the Indians during the past year. Cattle, horses, burros and mules daily are reported missing." At first the miners and ranchers responded by organizing private militia that were financed by local donations and staffed by volunteers after the territorial legislature narrowly defeated a bill to finance three ranger companies. Staffed by men such as Primativo Cervantes, whose prowess as an Indian fighter was known in Prescott, these units rode out from the towns and mining camps much like King Woolsey and his men had done, to retaliate for Indian livestock raids and attacks on isolated miners and travelers. In November 1868, the residents of Wickenburg contributed $2,000 to finance a militia outfit. However, as it became apparent that such private armies were inadequate, and that local residents could provide only limited funds for their operation, miners and businessmen in central Arizona began petitioning the federal government for military protection.

The first military post to be established in the region was Fort Whipple, opened in December 1863 in the Chino Valley and then moved in 1864 to Granite Creek, on the outskirts of the new town of Prescott. In 1865 and 1866, soldiers were briefly stationed in Wickenburg, although the town was never formally declared a post. Also during that time, troops were stationed at a temporary camp on Date Creek, about twenty-five miles north of Wickenburg and situated on the road from Prescott to La Paz and Ehrenberg. In 1867, as warfare with the Yavapai intensified, the army established a permanent post at Date Creek. At first called Camp McPherson, the post was soon rechristened Camp Date Creek and served as the local command headquarters for most military activities involving the western Yavapai.

Initially the army fought the Indians much as the miners and ranchers had done: whenever Yavapai attacked a miner's camp or traveling party, or raided for livestock, the troops were sent out on punitive expeditions. In addition, the soldiers patrolled roads and escorted parties of travelers in areas subject to frequent Indian attack. However, the expeditions and patrols had little impact, and the Yavapai continued to harass the Anglos and Mexican Americans moving into the region. To most of these new arrivals, the number of soldiers was far below what conditions seemed to dictate, and they kept up a drumbeat of criticism aimed at persuading territorial and federal officials to devote more resources to fighting Indians.

Although miners and settlers wanted to exterminate the Yavapai, the federal government hoped to persuade the Indians to settle on reservations. In 1865, shortly after Arizona's first Indian reservation was established along the Colorado River, some of the western Yavapai agreed to abandon their traditional migratory existence and move to the reservation along with other western Arizona tribes. However, the government provided inadequate rations at the reservation, and the Yavapai soon resumed their seasonal trips to the mountains to gather food; eventually, they abandoned the reservation altogether.

Five years later, worn down by army raids on their *rancherias* and food stores, a group of about 350 western Yavapai sued for peace and asked to live near the army post at Date Creek as reservation Indians. In return for permission to do so, the Indians agreed to stay away from the public roads and to assist the army in arresting and punishing "renegades" who stole livestock or caused other trouble away from the post. In addition, these Yavapai were allowed to continue their subsistence activities in the nearby mountains. A year later, in 1871, Date Creek was declared a temporary reservation and each Yavapai living there was given a daily ration of one pound of corn and one pound of beef. That same year, a second reservation for the Yavapai was established on the Verde River, near an army post there. The Rio Verde reservation, as it was called, was primarily occupied by south-eastern Yavapai.

Even as the population of these two reservations increased, how-ever, guerrilla warfare between Yavapai and the newcomers to central Arizona continued. On 5 November 1871, a party of men reported to be Yavapai warriors attacked a stagecoach traveling west from Wickenburg, killing six persons and badly wounding two others, one of whom soon died. Unlike other such attacks, this one attracted na-tional attention, for one of the slain passengers was Frederick Loring, a well-known journalist who had been traveling with an army survey party in the territory. At the time, some local residents claimed the holdup was not the work of Yavapai but of men who had disguised themselves as Indians; while some pointed fingers at a local Mexican "bandit," Inocensio Valenzuela, others thought they saw the handi-work of Charles Stanton, the owner of a store on Antelope Creek with a reputation for violent behavior.

Whichever the case—each view has its partisans today—the Wick-enburg, or Loring, Massacre had a chilling effect on relations with the Yavapai. From the perspective of those who favored a peaceful resolution of Indian-white conflict, the timing of the incident could not have been worse. Shortly before, military activities in the terri-tory had been suspended while Vincent Colyer, a peace commissioner appointed by President Ulysses Grant, attempted to negotiate with the Yavapai and Apaches to persuade them to move to reservations, some of which Colyer established while in the territory. With Yavapai from the Date Creek reservation implicated in the stage attack, the incident placed the conciliators on the defensive and galvanized pub-lic opinion in favor of a vigorous army campaign against the Yavapai and Apaches.

Meanwhile, the territory had a new army commander, Gen. George Crook, who immediately began preparing for a multi-front offensive against the remaining non-reservation Indians in the territory, and in particular against the Yavapai. In December 1871, Crook ordered all Yavapai not on a reservation to report to the Rio Verde reservation by February 1872; if they did not, he warned, they would be considered hostile and hunted down. However, just as Crook was about to launch his offensive, a second peace mission came to Arizona under the leadership of Gen. Oliver Otis Howard. Unlike Colyer before him, though, Howard concluded that force was the only way to subdue the warring bands, and he also approved Crook's proposal that once hostilities resumed, Indian scouts should be used by the army.

In September 1872, after months of waiting and preparation, Crook began his campaign against the Yavapai. His immediate prey were the Date Creek Yavapai allegedly responsible for the Wickenburg stage attack, who had fled the reservation and now were hiding in the upper reaches of the Santa Maria River, on the northern edges of their traditional homeland. An army contingent caught up with them at Muchos Canyon later that fall, and in the ensuing battle more than forty Yavapai were killed and large stores of food seized by the soldiers. This battle, which was costly given the small number of Indians at large in western Arizona, effectively ended the organized resistance of the western Yavapai. In December, army troops fought a deadly battle with the Yavapai at a cave along the Salt River in the Superstition Mountains—some accounts call it Skeleton or Skull Cave—in which between fifty and seventy-five Indians were killed. This battle, which mostly involved southeastern Yavapai, is remembered by the Yavapai as the most catastrophic event in their history.

By the end of the year, Yavapai resistance was effectively crushed. The next year, 1873, saw the closure of Camp Date Creek and the transfer of the Yavapai living there—about eight hundred persons—to the Rio Verde reservation. By the end of 1873, about a thousand Yavapai were living on the reservation, where they built irrigation ditches and began to farm. However, two years later, partly at the urging of ration contractors who did not like the Indians' growing self-sufficiency, the government closed the Rio Verde reservation and relocated the Yavapai to the San Carlos reservation, hitherto occupied solely by Apaches.

With this relocation, the Yavapai people became the only Indians in Arizona to be completely removed from their traditional homeland. Just as the miners, ranchers, and settlers had wanted, central Arizona—the Hassayampa and Verde river valleys, the Bradshaws and other mountain ranges—had been scoured clean of its original inhabitants. Eventually Indians returned to the Hassayampa valley. However, most of them were not Yavapai but Maricopas, who once were traditional enemies of the Yavapai. At least through the first decade of this century, Maricopas periodically journeyed from their homes along the Gila River to the Wickenburg area, where they hunted, picked cactus fruit, and mined clay for pottery.

The Decline of the Vulture Mine

Ironically, at about the same time that Wickenburg's residents were celebrating the successful conclusion of the war against the Yavapai, the owners of the Vulture Mine were fighting a losing battle to salvage their investment and keep the mine operating. In December 1871, the Vulture Mining Company sank a new shaft that struck a promising ore body at a depth of 240 feet, thus appearing to ensure the continued operation of the mine. However, as the miners continued excavating, they struck water at the 310-foot level. The mine flooded, forcing the owners to suspend operations while they attempted to raise enough capital to buy new pumps and resume work on the shaft. The timing for this setback could not have been worse. Depression struck the country in 1873, cutting off most sources of investment capital, and the Vulture Mining Company failed to raise the needed funds. By the end of the year, the Vulture was closed.

In 1874, a year after the Vulture was shut down by the company, Maricopa County officials seized the mine as compensation for the failure of the Vulture Mining Company to pay its taxes. When the county tried to sell the mine, to recover the $1,025 in delinquent taxes, it could find no takers. Over the next few years, various parties made sporadic attempts to reopen the Vulture, but no one succeeded in reviving the mine on anywhere near the scale of previous operations. For the most part, development work was confined to reprocessing the tailings left by earlier excavations. In fact, from this point on, much of the work done at the Vulture Mine would consist of reprocessing rather than new extraction.

One such reprocessing enterprise was established south of Wickenburg, at a point along the Hassayampa about ten miles downriver that eventually became known as Seymour. It was here that a ten-stamp mill had been successfully processing tailings from the Vulture Mine since moving to the site in 1872 from its original location near Wickenburg. The mill, which was owned by several Wickenburg residents including P. W. Smith and Frederick Brill and was popularly known as Smith's Mill, had a work force of about 130 men in 1878 and paid out average wages of $70 per month—a substantial sum of money in a cash-starved region such as the Hassayampa valley. One important reason for the mill's relocation was that the area around Wickenburg had been picked clean of firewood by woodcutters hired by the mining companies; near Seymour, untouched stands of mesquite promised a cheaper and more reliable source of the firewood needed to run the mill's steam power plant and amalgamation oven. However, just as Wickenburg's fortunes were hostage to the Vulture Mine, so were Seymour's. When a new group of owners acquired the Vulture in 1878 and built a mill at the mine itself, rather than along the river, the supply of ore to Smith's Mill was cut off. By 1880, the mill had been dismantled, and over the next few years, most of Seymour's residents drifted away to other communities.

The 1878 purchase of the Vulture Mine by the Central Arizona Mining Company at first seemed to promise renewed life for the gold mine. Formed specifically to reopen the Vulture, the Central Arizona Mining Company was rumored to have paid as much as $200,000 to buy out existing mining claims in the area of the mine. After selling stock on the basis of claims that over $2 million in gold reserves awaited extraction from the Vulture, the Central Arizona set about doing what no previous developer of the mine had managed to accomplish: process the ore at the mine itself, rather than at mills located along the Hassayampa River. This required construction of not only a new stamp mill but also a pipeline to carry river water up to the mine site. The pipeline, assembled from sheet iron and riveted by hand, was ten miles long and included a novel feature: taps installed at periodic intervals to prevent thirsty travelers and miners from puncturing the pipe to obtain water. The project was completed by 1880, as was the stamp mill and a steam-powered pumping plant used to lift the river water uphill to the mine.

In 1881, the first year after completing these ambitious capital improvements, the Central Arizona reported a profit from its operations at the Vulture. However, within a year, the company was losing money and struggling, as had its predecessors, with management turnover. More importantly, its claims of substantial ore reserves were being questioned in the mining press. One publication, the *Engineering and Mining Journal,* went so far as to advise its readers that "the public should carefully examine into the merits of this property ... and not give any attention to much that enters print relative to the mine." Although the Central Arizona reported that it had taken $210,000 in gold out of the Vulture in 1883, it still lost money owing to the high costs of maintaining its mill and pumping system. A year later, the company closed the Vulture Mine.

Wickenburg Struggles to Survive

Not surprisingly, the first closure of the Vulture Mine in 1873 dealt a serious blow to Wickenburg. When a reporter for the San Francisco *Chronicle* visited the town in late March 1877, he found little to suggest the lively mining camp of earlier days: "It looks like a town in the 12th Century. There are still a few men and women remaining in the ruined place. . . .There is an old mill here, but its wheels have long been silent, the rust has consumed the iron and the worm worked in the wood. The six hundred men who once labored here and spent their money with little care are gone, and memories alone remain."

Still, Wickenburg refused to die. What saved the town from complete abandonment was its location at the point where the road from the Colorado River town of Ehrenberg split, one branch of the road heading north to Prescott, the other branch heading south past the White Tank Mountains to the Southern Pacific rail line and the farming communities along the Salt and Gila rivers (Phoenix, Florence, and other towns). This brought a modest but steady stream of business to Wickenburg, in the form of freighters stopping for supplies and passengers on the California and Arizona Stage Company alighting for meals and lodging.

In an 1878 guidebook to the territory, Wickenburg was described as a town of about two hundred residents but only seven businesses: a hotel, two restaurants, two stores, a stage station, and a telegraph station, most fronting on Center Street (now Wickenburg Way). The Vulture Mine's forty-stamp mill was still silent, and the town of Vulture, which had grown up around the mill just north of Wickenburg, consisted of fewer than thirty adobe buildings "in which but few persons now live."

When federal census-takers arrived in the Hassayampa River valley in 1880, they found only 104 persons in Wickenburg, with a few hundred more living in the surrounding area. When the first business directory for Arizona was published a year later, in 1881, Wickenburg was credited with only six businesses: a blacksmith, a general merchandise dealer, two hotels, a saloon and feed yard, and a Wells Fargo agency. As during earlier downturns in the 1870s, the patronage of stage passengers and freighters traveling along the Phoenix-California-Prescott road supplemented the modest trade provided by local residents, helping to keep the town's businesses alive.

When a reporter for the *Arizona Gazette,* a Phoenix newspaper, passed through Wickenburg en route to the Harcuvar Mountains, he found little evidence of the prosperous mining camp of earlier days. "Here are one hundred empty houses, many in good condition and hotels, dwellings, saloons, dance-halls—all deserted," he wrote. "The present population may be counted on the fingers of both hands, and even the very atmosphere of the place bears an air of expectation; a sort of waiting for better times." As he noted, the town's hopes still rested on a revival of local mining activities. A recent discovery of lead ore seemed promising, the reporter advised his readers, and local residents expected other mineral discoveries as well.

Life in Wickenburg

Although Wickenburg was known to most Arizonans as a mining community, what sustained the town during these difficult years was farming. Centuries of periodic floods had deposited rich soil along the banks of the Hassayampa River, in a narrow river bottom that extended for several miles up and down the river from Wickenburg. The Yavapai had cultivated pumpkins and squash in the river bottom, and the Anglos and Mexicans who came with the first mining rush soon grew a wide variety of crops almost year-round.

When a reporter for the *Arizona Miner* visited Wickenburg in 1870, he found local farmers raising grains such as barley, wheat, and corn; alfalfa for hay; potatoes; sorghum; vegetables; and fruits such as grapes, peaches, apples, quinces, plums, and pears. The farms he described were not very large; the largest single field he saw was seventy acres (planted in barley), and most were no larger than a dozen acres. Because the land away from the river was suitable only for light grazing, Wickenburg's farms were confined to the river bottom. Another factor limiting the size of farms was the need for periodic irrigation. Every Wickenburg farm had its own network of ditches that diverted water directly from the river or, when the river was not flowing, distributed water brought to the surface by wells dug into the water table lying just under the river bottom. These irrigation systems were simple in design and construction—most farmers used pumps powered by mules to raise their well water—but they nevertheless required considerable time and labor to maintain.

Of course, each farm had its own livestock as well—horses, mules, cattle, and sheep. And when the Vulture Mine was operating, large numbers of mules and oxen were kept in the river valley to pull the wagons that hauled ore, water, fuel, and other supplies to and from the mine. Otherwise, though, it does not appear that ranching was a major activity in Wickenburg during the 1870s and 1880s.

From the limited evidence available today, it seems clear that only a few of the farms and ranches around Wickenburg were run as commercial enterprises. Henry Wickenburg and Frederick Brill, two of Wickenburg's more substantial farmers, sold grain, produce, and fruit not only in Wickenburg but also in Prescott and other mining communities in central Arizona. However, most of the farms in the Wickenburg area were devoted to subsistence farming, that is, raising enough food for the families who lived there, with perhaps a modest surplus that could be sold or bartered for household goods and foodstuffs that were not raised locally. From time to time, a family might augment its income with wage labor—in mining, construction, or on other farms and ranches, as the local economy permitted—and with occasional sales of livestock.

Many of these families were Mexican Americans who had been attracted to the region for its mining prospects but had stayed to establish farms and ranches along the river. According to the 1880 census, just under half the population in the Wickenburg area had Spanish surnames—a figure that could well have been too low, given the historical tendency of census-takers to undercount minorities, especially those whose primary language was not English. After all, descriptions of Wickenburg written during this period by travelers and newspaper reporters consistently emphasized the Hispanic character of the town.

For that matter, the tendency of these visitors to describe Wickenburg as a "relic of the past" in part reflected a prejudice against Mexican Americans that was endemic to Arizona during this time. To most Anglos living in the territory, Mexican-American communities seemed sleepy, run-down, indolent, and lacking in ambition. Thus, many Anglo visitors who were accustomed to busier towns such as Prescott, Phoenix, and Tucson described Wickenburg's small-scale farm and ranch economy as moribund, even dying. However, as Mexicans and Mexican Americans in similar communities elsewhere in the Southwest had been demonstrating for years, such an economy was well-suited to an arid land with limited resources. Most importantly, it was sustainable in ways that allowed a small but stable community to survive in Wickenburg regardless of whether local mines were producing or not.

One sign of this stability was the establishment, in 1879, of the town's first school. That year, local residents petitioned the territory to form

Maricopa County School District No. 9, to serve the children of Wickenburg, Vulture Mine, and Seymour. By the spring of 1880, the school's average daily attendance was eighteen. The next year, a second district was established at the Vulture Mine, but the school was open for only four months before closing for good. Few school records from these early years of the district have survived, so it is not clear how long the school year was or how many children were enrolled. During the 1884–85 school year, the first for which full records exist, ten students were taught by a single teacher in a house owned by one of the district's three trustees. With revenues of $368 and expenditures of $240, the district was hard-pressed for funds; when the teacher, who was paid $75 per month, quit in the middle of the term, the trustees closed the school for the year. The next year, the school went through three teachers and was closed for two months of the year owing to a lack of both teacher and funds. Between 1885 and 1887, enrollments at the one-room school remained low, fluctuating between four and twelve children.

As the difficulties faced by the school district suggest, Wickenburg in the 1880s was a thinly populated, poor town dependent for its livelihood on the modest produce of its small ranches and farms, and the sporadic and unreliable production of local mines. The town was not incorporated, so there was no local government and no local law enforcement. For the latter, Wickenburg residents relied on the Maricopa County sheriff's office, headquartered in Phoenix—still at least a day's travel away. The town lacked other important institutions as well; it had no church building, theater, bank, newspaper, or fraternal organizations.

If the business owners and residents of Wickenburg were waiting for the revival of local mines to stimulate their town's economy, they surely were disappointed. Miners continued to discover new prospects in the nearby mountains, but few made good on their claims, lacking either sufficient paying ore or adequate development capital. The Vulture Mine continued to frustrate its owners, who found that with each attempt to reopen the mine, the assessments of its future prospects grew more pessimistic. In 1888, after owning the mine and some adjacent claims for only a year, Colorado silver baron Horace A. W. Tabor sold the Vulture to the Kaiser Gold Mining Company, an English concern that extracted from Tabor a promise that he would refund the purchase price if the company was not satisfied with the mine's output. After trying for several months to resume operations at the Vulture, the company hired a Cornish mining engineer to examine the mine. James Morrish's report, which described the Vulture as being in "a state of confusion and disorder" and "a most disreputable condition from top to bottom," charged that its reserves had been exaggerated and recommended against its purchase. Kaiser eventually got its money back from Tabor, in 1892, but only after taking him to court for refusing to honor his initial agreement.

The Walnut Grove Dam Disaster

While the Kaiser Company and Horace Tabor were arguing over the Vulture in court, Wickenburg was stunned by a disaster worse than any that Arizona had seen before: the rupture of a dam on the Hassayampa River at Walnut Grove, about thirty miles upstream from Wickenburg. When the dam broke on 22 February 1890, it unleashed a wall of churning water that surged down the riverbed with such force that it uprooted mature trees, sending them rocketing down the river as if they were merely matchsticks. The break occurred early in the morning, at about 2 a.m., after heavy rains in the Hassayampa's watershed had swelled the lake past the point where the earth-and-rubble dam could safely contain the water. Employees of the company that had built the structure, the Walnut Grove Water Storage Company, noticed fissures in the dam several hours before the break, and sent a man downriver with instructions to wake river-bottom residents and get them to higher ground. However, according to local reports, the messenger stopped at a tavern not far below the dam, where he stayed to drink for several hours, and so failed to carry out his mission. As a result, the miners and settlers asleep in their homes and camps along the river bottom were caught unawares by the flood, which swept everything in its path downriver. Some heard the rumble of approaching water and scrambled to safety, but many others were carried away. Exactly how many persons died that night is unknown. At the time, estimates of the dead were as high as seventy, with many newspapers suggesting that the toll would never be determined. More recently, one historian has concluded that thirty-eight persons were killed and an additional fourteen were declared missing.

In addition to the tremendous loss of life, the physical damage to the river bottom was substantial. "[Over] the entire distance between Seymour and the main dam[,] a scene of indescribable desolation presented itself," the *Arizona Gazette* reported in its initial story on the disaster. "At or near Wickenburg all the ranches were totally destroyed, Brill's house was the only one left." Two days later, the newspaper's correspondent wrote, "The canyon as far down as has been explored presents a scene of desolation which no pen can describe, and when the awful result becomes known [it] will be terrible to contemplate. . . .[T]he canyon for a distance of thirty-five miles is strewn with bedding, dead horses, cattle and hogs, broken wagons, and in fact everything used by the settlers in the valley."

In Wickenburg, the flood's impact was felt by everyone. In addition to carrying off many of the ranch and farm buildings located in the river bottom, the flood also stripped away much of the valuable soil that had made Hassayampa farms so productive, as well as many of the fruit trees that had been planted there. The town's farms never recovered from this blow, and in later years their output was only a fraction of what it had been before the flood. Several property owners, including Henry Wickenburg, sued the dam company in an attempt to recover damages suffered by their farms. However, the lawsuit, which was heard in Maricopa County courts, was dismissed on the grounds that it should have been filed in Yavapai County, where the dam was located. The plaintiffs never refiled the suit.

The events surrounding the flood also cast a harsh light on the divisions that existed in Wickenburg between the Anglo and Mexican-American communities. According to the *Arizona Gazette*, the brunt of the flood's impact was borne by the Mexican Americans, whose homes lay closer to the river. "The country is inhabited by

Mexican herders and miners, and the loss of life sustained by those people will in all human probability never be known," its correspondent wrote. As bodies were retrieved from the riverbed and the extent of casualties became known, the paper published the names of all the Anglo Americans who had died but said only that "seven Mexicans and eight Chinamen" had been killed. When it came time to bury the victims of the flood, some of whom were never positively identified, the Mexicans Americans and Chinese were refused burial in the town's cemetery. Responding to this affront, Ygnacio Garcia, a local rancher, donated some of his land for their burial. Later named the Garcia Cemetery, it remains an important town landmark.

Given its severity, the flood could easily have been the final blow to the town's hopes for survival. Now, in addition to seeing its principal mine closed due to poor management and high operating costs, the town had lost perhaps its most precious asset: the rich river-bottom soil that had sustained its farms and ranches. Despite these problems, though, Wickenburg's residents stayed. For many—and especially for the Mexican Americans who made up much of the town's population—leaving was an option that offered little; after all, Wickenburg was their home. As for the town's small business community, it clung to the old hope that another mine like the Vulture might bring new prosperity to the town. Even if that failed to happen, the town's residents reasoned, they would benefit from the money that mining investors always seemed willing to spend on development work. With the river-bottom farms wiped out, Wickenburg was once again a mining town.

4   A Mining Community
   Searches for a New Identity

As THE NEW CENTURY APPROACHED, Wickenburg appeared to have come full circle in the thirty years since the discovery of the Vulture Mine. With its valuable river-bottom farmland all but destroyed by the Walnut Grove Dam flood, the town found itself once again dependent on mining to support its small population and modest business community. For a time beginning in the late 1890s, the discovery and development of mining prospects kept pace with the area's hopes for new growth, and the town's business owners were hopeful the growth would be permanent. "We feel that we have a mining district that will, in the near future, become one of the richest and best known mineral producing sections in the West," L. C. Nickerson wrote in a promotional pamphlet published in 1905 by the Wickenburg Business Men and Miners' Association.

Yet despite the optimism of Nickerson and his fellow promoters, the mining economy in the Wickenburg area never quite realized its promise. The region saw much investment in mines, but little significant production, and when major mineral discoveries were made, such as at Congress, they brought only indirect economic benefits. Still, the success of the Congress Mine did help bring the railroad to Wickenburg, which along with other changes helped lay the groundwork for the eventual diversification of the town's economy. These changes were slow to take place, and they were not always apparent to visitors and new arrivals, who still tended to see little more than a dusty mining town when they first alighted from the train. But by the end of the First World War, Wickenburg had acquired a growing ranching economy to ease its dependence on mining, incorporated and formed its first municipal government, and taken its first steps toward acquiring such urban amenities as a newspaper, water system, electricity, and telephones.

Survey of the Townsite

Wickenburg's first step toward true permanency—something that no territorial mining town could take for granted—was made in 1895, when the town's residents voted at a special school board meeting to erect the town's first district-owned schoolhouse. Since forming the school district in 1879, the trustees had rented classroom space from various property owners in town rather than erect their own building. Faced with criticism that the most recently occupied schoolhouse, for which they paid $7 a month, was unsafe, the trustees decided to tear down an abandoned building at the Vulture Mine and rebuild it on a lot in Wickenburg provided by Ygnacio Garcia, whose earlier generosity had given the town the cemetery that later bore his name. In the nineteen years since his arrival in Wickenburg, the former miner had established himself as one of the area's more successful ranchers and served on the local school board at least since 1884. With the donated land and volunteer labor, the project cost the district only $50. The "new" structure was the first building owned by the school district, and it remained Wickenburg's only schoolhouse for the next ten years.

Although Wickenburg by now was more than thirty years old, the town actually had no legal standing in the territory. For one reason or another, Henry Wickenburg had failed to formally survey the townsite and record the plat at the county recorder's office. To remedy this defect, which cast a pall over every landowner's title, Wickenburg hired P. C. Bicknell to formally survey the townsite in February 1897 and record a plat map with Maricopa County. With a proper townsite patent in hand, the town's property owners could now take advantage of the growth they felt sure was coming. "Wickenburg was a prosperous place several years ago, but when mining in that section came to a standstill, so did Wickenburg," the *Arizona Republican,* a Phoenix newspaper, observed when it reported the new survey. "When the old mines started up again and new ones began to be opened, Wickenburg commenced to move again and gives promise of eclipsing its former career of activity."

The Arrival of the Railroad

The greatest change to come to Wickenburg in the 1890s was the construction of a rail line connecting the town with Prescott and Ash Fork, to the north, and Phoenix, to the south. For years, area business owners and promoters had been urging construction of a rail line to serve the mines and communities of the Bradshaw Mountains and Hassayampa River valley. In 1886, the Prescott & Arizona Central Railroad was formed and a line constructed from Prescott north to Ash Fork, where it connected with the Atlantic & Pacific Railroad's transcontinental line. Much to the dismay of Wickenburg residents, when the Prescott & Arizona Central began making plans to extend the line southward, its directors chose a route through the Black Canyon, on the opposite side of the Bradshaw Mountains from the town.

It was at this point, in the late 1880s, that a rivalry developed between the Prescott & Arizona Central and a group of investors led by Frank Murphy and Joseph "Diamond Joe" Reynolds, who were working to develop a new mine called the Congress, located a few miles north of Wickenburg. Without rail service, the mine's future was uncertain owing to high transportation costs; with a rail connection, the costs of importing machinery and other goods would be dramatically lowered and the mine rendered much more profitable. Consequently, Murphy's group began pushing for a Prescott-to-Phoenix rail line that would serve the Congress Mine. At first they attempted to buy the Prescott & Arizona Central, which they planned to extend to Phoenix via Wickenburg. When their purchase offer was rebuffed,

Murphy and his fellow investors formed their own rail line, the Santa Fe, Prescott & Phoenix Railroad, in 1891. Engineers for the SFP&P mapped out a line that would run from Ash Fork to Prescott, then southwest to Congress, through Wickenburg, and on to Phoenix. Construction on the south end of the line began in Phoenix in October 1891, and on the north end in Ash Fork in January 1892. By the end of 1894, the tracks had reached Wickenburg; in March 1895, the north and south ends were linked and service from Ash Fork to Phoenix was inaugurated with ceremonies in the capital city.

At first, the economic impact of the new railroad on Wickenburg was relatively modest. Among all the shipping points along the SFP&P, which was quickly dubbed the Peavine because of the twisting route it followed through the mountains, Wickenburg recorded the least amount of business during the railroad's early years. In 1895, 1,220 tons of freight were shipped into Wickenburg and 490 shipped out, for a net revenue of $913. The following year, 4,191 tons of freight were unloaded at the Wickenburg depot while only 971 tons were loaded, for a net profit to the railroad of less than $2,000.

Nevertheless, the long-term impact of the railroad was significant. Without railroad service, Wickenburg's tourist industry might not have emerged in the 1920s, nor would its budding ranch economy have been able to expand as it did during the early decades of the century—two developments that helped secure the economic future of the town and its surrounding communities. Wickenburg's residents knew very well that towns bypassed by the railroad faced great odds in maintaining lively business districts, and that losing a rail connection often meant the death of a small community such as theirs. That the Santa Fe, Prescott & Phoenix had chosen Wickenburg as a depot location represented a vote of confidence in the town that its inhabitants greatly needed. It also brought tangible benefits in the form of jobs. As the railroad's physical presence increased—it eventually built a depot (completed in 1895), section house, water tank, pump house, and employee housing facilities in Wickenburg—the number of residents with railroad jobs went up as well. By 1910, nearly one out of ten jobs in the Wickenburg area was provided by the railroad, with even more accounted for by seasonal labor and construction work on the railroad.

The Congress and Other Local Mines

As the freight receipts of the Santa Fe, Prescott & Phoenix make clear, mining was still the backbone of Wickenburg's economy, just as it was for Prescott and most of the communities scattered across the Bradshaw Mountains and along the Hassayampa River valley. Almost all of the railroad's freight revenue earned north of the Salt River Valley came from mining, while most of its business in the Phoenix area came from agricultural shipments. In fact, shipments to and from Congress Junction (where a small spur line from the mine connected to the main line) and Jerome Junction (where a narrow-gauge line from the United Verde Company's copper mines in Jerome met the SFP&P) accounted for 96 percent of the railroad's earnings from the northern segment of its line.

The Congress Mine, located three miles northwest of Congress Junction, was discovered in the 1880s. However, except for some development work, little was done with the property during that decade. In 1887, the claims were purchased by Joseph "Diamond Joe" Reynolds, who began to develop the mine. After building a twenty-stamp mill and concentration facilities, Reynolds' managers found that most of the gold reserves at the mine could not be recovered profitably with the techniques then available to them. (The cyanide process of extracting gold was not yet perfected.) They managed to keep the mine running from 1889 to 1891, in the process leaving tailings rich enough to warrant reprocessing later on, but in 1891 they decided to shut it down to await arrival of the new railroad. Until that time, the mine's managers had been forced to ship ore by mule or ox team to Prescott, where it was then loaded onto Prescott & Arizona Central cars for a four- to five-day rail trip to the main Atlantic & Pacific line at Ash Fork—a costly and time-consuming exercise.

Reynolds died in 1891, and Frank Murphy, then the mine's superintendent, took over ownership with several other investors and formed the Congress Gold Company. With their own railroad, the SFP&P, providing faster and cheaper transportation, the mine was reopened in 1891 and operated continuously until 1911. In 1895, a roasting and cyaniding plant was constructed, thus allowing the company to reprocess the tailings from its earlier work and to recover gold from ore that hitherto had been left in the ground. By 1901, when the company was reorganized as the Congress Consolidated Mines Company, it had a work force of 450 men. Profits grew along with production. In its first three years of operation, from 1889 to 1891, the Congress yielded just under $600,000 in net returns. Between 1894 and 1911, when the Congress was closed down, it produced more than $7 million in net revenue. The community that grew up around the mine, which was divided into two sections known as Mill Town and Lower Town, had its own post office, stores, saloons, and cemetery. In 1900, almost a thousand persons lived in Congress and Congress Junction; by 1910, with the mine on the verge of being shut down, the town's population had dropped by half, to less than five hundred.

What the Congress' success meant for Wickenburg is hard to say. With its own rail stop for shipping goods in and ore out, and its own small mercantile community, the town's miners and their families probably did much of their business in Congress. Still, Wickenburg was the closest community with anything resembling a full array of services, and Wickenburg's business owners probably received a modest but steady flow of business from mine workers, managers, and visitors. Certainly Wickenburg residents had the Congress to thank for the railroad, which likely would have been puffing its way up and down the Black Canyon had Frank Murphy and his confederates not had such a powerful incentive to bring a railroad into the Hassayampa valley.

The Last Gasp of the Vulture

The emergence of the Congress as a major gold-producing mine—brief as its productive life was—could not have come at a better time for Wickenburg, for the traditional mainstay of the area's economy, the Vulture Mine, was nearing the end of its productive life. Still under the ownership of Colorado silver baron Horace Tabor, the Vulture had effectively been closed since 1884. The Walnut Grove Dam flood had wiped out part of the pipeline built in the early 1880s, again depriving the property of a convenient water supply, and Tabor had come close to losing the mine to a tax judgment soon thereafter. While Tabor continued to try to sell the mine, a lessee set up a modest cyanide processing facility and reworked the mine tailings; he even tore down some of the earliest buildings and processed their stone walls, which contained more gold than most of the ore taken out of the mine in the last two decades.

Finally, Tabor surrendered to the inevitable and abandoned the mine. In 1897, the Vulture was sold at a tax sale to the newly formed Vulture Mining Company, which was financed by midwestern investors and managed by Tucson banker W. C. Davis. The new firm intended to set up a larger, more comprehensive cyanide processing system, but it soon succumbed to the same problems that had defeated its predecessors: lack of water, high operating costs, and crippling debt. The mine was again closed, and it remained shuttered except for a nine-year period beginning in 1908, when an estimated $1.8 million in gold was taken out.

Over the years, various historians have attempted to explain why the Vulture, despite its fame and reputed richness, never quite lived up to its potential. One common explanation is that the mine was in fact richer than its official production figures suggested. "It is claimed that a great quantity of bullion was taken out of which no trace or account was ever found," James M. Barney wrote in the 1930s, after interviewing longtime residents and former prospectors and miners. According to Barney, laborers hauling ore from the mine to the riverside mills routinely stole high-grade ore from the wagons, making up the weight loss with rocks picked up along the road. Supervision at the mine was "very lax," Barney claimed, allowing miners to carry ore directly out of the shaft. "An organized system of robbery seemed to be prevalent," he concluded, one in which virtually all of the employees—millers, foremen, and miners—conspired to steal from the "owners in the East."

As is often the case with such claims, they remain unprovable one way or the other; thieves never leave written records. But while there is no denying that "high-grading" (the practice of stealing high-grade ore) was a problem at the Vulture just as it was at every other precious metal mine in the West, there is a more prosaic explanation for the Vulture's fitful productivity: the mine's vein simply was not as rich as its boosters claimed. It was a problematic mine from the beginning. The principal vein did contain valuable ore, but it was fractured at several points and kept disappearing from the miners, forcing them to spend valuable time and money relocating it. More to the point, the Vulture was hobbled by high operating costs—for transportation, fuel, water, and food—and the lack of a reliable, nearby water source. And every owner after Henry Wickenburg—the only owner not to pay a large sum of money for the mine—had to contend with debt costs as well. With all these disadvantages, it is not surprising that the Vulture was only intermittently profitable. According to historian Duane Smith, contemporary engineering reports and other sober estimates suggest that the total production of the Vulture over its lifetime was between $4 million and $6 million—a handsome sum, but not the $10 million to $30 million (or even more) figures that sometimes find their way into stories about Arizona's first large gold mine.

Ironically, while investors may never have been satisfied with the Vulture Mine, the people of Wickenburg—especially local miners and business owners—must have known that in its own way, the Vulture was indeed very productive. Its discovery did more to advertise Arizona and the Hassayampa region than any other mining development at the time, and its reported riches helped bring prospectors, residents, and investors to a territory that only a few years before had been regarded as an arid wasteland suitable only for jackrabbits. More importantly, the Vulture brought a steady stream of investment capital into Wickenburg, providing jobs, supporting businesses, and attracting services—the telegraph, wagon road, and later railroad—that helped the town survive and eventually prosper. The mine not only led to the founding of Wickenburg and other local communities; it also helped stimulate the settlement of Phoenix by providing manpower and a reliable market for the Salt River Valley's infant farms and hayfields.

Renewed Interest in Wickenburg's Mines

When the Vulture Mine's demise came, it was noted quietly and without fanfare, not only because it was expected but also because other mines and mine prospects in the area were attracting more attention. "Wickenburg is awakening from its long Rip Van Winkle lethargy," the *Arizona Gazette* reported in 1901. "After twenty years uneventful in stirring news, the camp is again alive and its people are filled with buoyancy at future possibilities." According to a 1905 promotional booklet published by the Wickenburg Business Men and Miners' Association, ninety-four mining companies or groups of mines operated in the area, many of them holding more than one property. However, virtually all of the mines were either prospects or in development; few had yielded paying ore in sufficient quantities to justify calling them producing mines.

Typical of these newer enterprises was Oro Grande Mines, owned by George B. Upton, who held fourteen mining claims north of town, as well as water rights on the Hassayampa River. Upton and his work crew built an "experimental" ten-stamp mill and a pumping plant and pipeline that fed storage tanks at his main mine site, as well as two boarding houses, several dwellings, a barn, club room, cookhouse, carpenter's shop, powder magazine, hoist house with changing room, and other outbuildings. Using machinery powered by gasoline engines, the miners had sunk a 340-foot main shaft and excavated more than a mile of adits, stopes, and other passages. As impressive as the work at the Oro Grande was, though, Upton's mine was still in the development stage.

Although Upton's mine was not fully productive, at least it yielded promising ore; other prospects never even made it that far. Around

1910, a self-taught mining engineer named Frank Crampton arrived in Wickenburg to manage the Copper Belt, an idle gold mine owned by a New York architect. On first appearance, the Copper Belt seemed to be a good prospect. "The tent houses and frame buildings looked as if they belonged to a large operating mine," Crampton later wrote. "The office building was huge and contained fully equipped assaying and engineering offices. Every tool imaginable was in either the black-smith shop or tool shed." On closer inspection, however, he and an associate found the mine to be less impressive. The stamp mill needed twenty thousand dollars in machinery before it could function, Crampton concluded, and "there was no evidence of any work hav-ing been performed underground." Overall, Crampton did not like what he saw: "What we found followed the same pattern as that of hundreds of other good prospects. It was an old story: promoters had mined the sucker-investors instead of ore."

Other than the Congress Mine, perhaps the most productive mine in the area was the Octave, which was located north of Wickenburg and about ten miles east of Congress Junction. The Octave Gold Min-ing Company was formed in the late 1890s, and regular production began about 1900. Over the next five years, miners took out an estimated $2 million in gold and silver, most of which was pro-cessed at the mine in the company's forty-stamp mill and cyaniding plant. In 1907, a new company acquired the mine and began operat-ing it with electricity generated at a plant constructed for that pur-pose in Wickenburg. Unfortunately, the company could not work the mine profitably and was forced to close the Octave in 1912.

Wickenburg at the Turn of the Century

Even if most of the mines around Wickenburg never yielded a ton of paying ore, they still were valuable to the town's residents and busi-ness owners; an operation such as the Oro Grande, for example, re-quired regular and frequent purchases of supplies and foodstuffs, much of which were bought locally, and maintained a payroll that brought spending miners into town on the weekends and holidays.

According to freight receipts from the Santa Fe, Prescott & Phoenix Railroad, the line's revenue from shipments *into* the mining districts of central Arizona was about double its income from shipments *out* of those districts. This represented a substantial investment by outsiders in the Wickenburg area, and it produced such ventures as the Arizona Sampling and Reduction Company, a small custom smelter that operated on the west side of town at least between 1905 and 1917. The company assayed and processed ore from the small mines around town, using not only time-honored methods such as concentration and amalgamation, but also newer ones such as flotation and cyaniding.

As mining investors, prospectors, and miners began arriving in larger numbers, business and construction activity in the town picked up. "Old adobes that were dilapidated and uninhabited are being repatched, replastered and renovated, new frame buildings are springing up in every direction, while the builders themselves are living in tents, a hundred or more of them being pitched all along this old Arizona town of Hassayampa fame," the *Arizona Gazette* reported in 1901. According to a Prescott newspaper, the *Courier*, town lots that year were selling for between $100 and $500, and the *Arizona Republican* claimed that Henry Wickenburg had sold $3,000 in town lots, enough to prompt him to plat the Wickenburg Addition to the original townsite.

In 1908, the town received a modest boost—probably little more than a few new railroad jobs—when the Arizona and California (A&C) Railroad was opened. This new line, known popularly as the Parker Cutoff, was a branch line owned by the Santa Fe Railroad that left the SFP&P tracks at a junction located just north of Wickenburg and passed through Parker, Arizona, en route to California. This gave the Santa Fe, which acquired full ownership of the A&C and SFP&P in 1911, a direct route from Phoenix to California.

In many respects, Wickenburg at the turn of the century was still a simple, rustic town. It had no permanent church building or library, no fraternal organizations, no bank, and no telephone or electricity, and it even lacked a substantial hotel that would appeal to tourists or business travelers. However, with its population increasing and renewed business activity in town, these deficiencies were soon remedied. In 1901 the town acquired its first newspaper, the *Wickenburg News-Herald,* which was started by Harriet Wilson and DeForest Hall. (Hall would later gain regional fame as Dick Wick Hall, the proprietor of and resident humorist in Salome, a small town on the railroad west of Wickenburg.) Although Wickenburg subsequently had trouble keeping the paper in town—the *News-Herald* was moved to Martinez in 1903—this nevertheless represented an important step forward for the business community, which needed some kind of publication to promote the town and its businesses. In 1904, a second paper, the *Miner,* was established under the ownership of Angela Hammer. Two years later, she bought the peripatetic *News-Herald,* which by then had moved back to Wickenburg. Combining the two newspapers, Hammer published the Wickenburg *Miner* until 1913, when she left town to start a newspaper in Casa Grande.

In 1902, the town's first telephone service was established, and for a time the system's exchange doubled as Wickenburg's first public library, which enjoyed a brief existence before closing for a number of years. (The operator was also the librarian.) Also about this time, the town's first church building, St. Anthony of Padua, was constructed in 1902 under the direction of Franciscan priests from Phoenix, who until then had conducted services in local homes. Because the congregation was a small one, the church continued to rely on visiting priests from Phoenix and then Prescott until 1942, when the town finally was made a parish. In 1905, Elizabeth Smith established the Vernetta Hotel in a handsome two-story brick building on Railroad Street (now Frontier Street) that was among the first sights to greet rail passengers when they arrived at the depot, which was across and just down the street from the hotel.

Smith, who was one of the town's few black residents, arrived in Wickenburg sometime around 1897. Before setting up the Vernetta, she and her husband William ran the Baxter Hotel on Center Street (now Wickenburg Way) and lived on a small farm along the river bottom. Cultivated and apparently well-educated, she was among the

founders of Wickenburg's first Protestant congregation, the First Presbyterian Church, established in 1905. Sources differ on how she came
to start her own hotel; some claim that the railroad, wanting to provide much-needed lodging and food for its passengers, approached
Smith with an offer to finance the venture if she would take charge of
it. Although racial prejudice eventually forced her to withdraw from
active involvement in community affairs, especially at the church she
helped found, many residents considered her an exemplary host and
the Vernetta to be the best hotel in town. When she died, the
Hassayampa Sun praised Smith for "her many deeds of kindness to
the community."

A year after Smith established the Vernetta, in 1906, the Brayton
Commercial Company, a general merchandise store on Railroad Street
that would be the commercial mainstay of Wickenburg for several
decades, was established. Although the original Brayton's building no
longer stands, the hotel building remains, a reminder of the time when
business was oriented toward the railroad. Another historic structure
that has survived from this period of development is the Wickenburg
Grammar School (later called the Garcia School), on Tegner Street.
Built in 1905 as a one-room schoolhouse, the simple brick building
was erected on land earlier donated to the school district by Ygnacio
Garcia. The $1,600 in bonds sold to finance the project were approved
41–2 by town residents, who later voted 36–29 to keep the school at its
then-current location rather than move it. When the new school
opened in January 1906, it had an enrollment of fifty-eight children.
The single teacher was paid $75 per month for a school year that lasted
between six and eight months, and actual attendance fluctuated
around forty students each day. In 1908, the school trustees voted to
divide the schoolhouse into two rooms and hire a second teacher so
that two grades could be taught at once—a major step given the
district's modest income of $954 that year.

By 1906, the town's business community included thirty-nine enterprises of various sizes, about one-fifth of them owned by Mexican
Americans. In most respects, Wickenburg remained a typical mining
town: saloons, general merchandise stores, boarding houses, and

blacksmith shops accounted for nearly half of the town's businesses. Still, residents could see that their community had grown sufficiently that the old informal practices of town management would no longer suffice, so in 1909 they decided to incorporate. Two months after voting 36–5 in favor of incorporation, the town's residents went to the polls to elect the new town's first officers. Henry Cowell was chosen mayor, while Felipe Garcia, R. W. Baxter, C. H. Widmeyer, and John Bachtiger were elected as members of the town council. To administer affairs in Wickenburg, the mayor and council appointed Edward L. Garcia as town marshal (at a monthly salary of $30), T. J Prescott as town attorney (for $42 a month), Ike B. Wood as constable, and John Riggs as justice of the peace.

Unfortunately, Henry Wickenburg never lived to see the organization of the town's first government. In 1865, two years after he started the Vulture Mine, Wickenburg had sold the most valuable part of his claim to a group of New York investors for $50,000—only half of which he actually received. Although he continued to dabble in mining after the sale, mainly by locating and then trying to sell other claims, Wickenburg at heart was a farmer. Until the Walnut Grove Dam flood in 1890, his riverside farm was known throughout the area for its fruit, potatoes, and other produce. A lifelong bachelor, Wickenburg was by all accounts a gruff but friendly man known for his generosity and, in his later years, his evident enjoyment at playing the role of resident old-timer. In 1905, in ill health and apparently despondent over finances, Henry Wickenburg retired to a grove of trees by the Hassayampa River and ended his life with a gunshot to the head.

New Growth for the Town

The decision to incorporate came during Wickenburg's first decade of significant population growth since its founding in the mid-1860s. In 1900, the town's population was 276, of whom more than half (143) were Mexican American. By the next census, in 1910, the population of Wickenburg had more than doubled, to 570 persons, of whom nearly half (237) were Mexican Americans. Were it not for the impending closure of the Congress Mine, which prompted about half the residents of Congress to leave by 1910, the area surrounding Wickenburg would have experienced a similar increase in population. Instead, after peaking at nearly two thousand in 1900, the area's population had dropped to 1,534—still a substantial number compared to twenty years before. As in the town, about half the area's residents were Mexican American.

The Wickenburg that railroad passengers and road travelers saw in 1915 was substantially different from the hamlet that had greeted stage passengers thirty years before. Reflecting the railroad's dominance of transportation, the town's main business street had shifted from the Phoenix-Prescott-Ehrenberg road (which followed Center and Tegner streets) to Railroad Street. The east side of Railroad was lined with a variety of businesses ranging from the two-story Vernetta Hotel to Brayton's sprawling store complex, which by then included a stable situated across the railroad tracks. Tegner at this time was little more than a back street; other than the Catholic church, a theater, livery stable, and automobile garage, the street contained only scattered dwellings and vacant lots. The town's primary residential area was situated immediately west of the railroad tracks, in the neat square blocks that now make up the older part of town. In addition, a good number of homes were scattered between the business area and the river. It was there, as well as on the ranches and farms scattered up and down the river bottom, that many of the town's longtime residents lived.

Wickenburg's new appearance reflected changes in the economic structure of the town and its surrounding area that had been underway since the new century began. The town's economy was diversifying. Although mining remained important, it was no longer the only significant source of employment and business. The railroad, which accounted for very few jobs at the turn of the century, by 1910 employed nearly fifty persons in and around Wickenburg, and it was responsible indirectly for additional jobs by providing seasonal work for carpenters and other skilled craftsmen. Aided by the railroad, the town's commercial and service businesses had increased not only in number but also in type; no longer were customers confined to a handful of choices as to where to take their business. The number of town jobs more than doubled between 1900 and 1910 and, most importantly, a noticeable expansion of the area's ranching and farming economy was underway.

Over the next decade, from 1910 to 1920, Wickenburg's population declined slightly, to 527 persons. Other developments in the community during the 1910–1920 decade, however, suggested increasing stability. In 1914, the town acquired its first bank, the Traders' Bank. Three years later, a town-owned water system was constructed, relieving residents of Wickenburg's central blocks of the necessity of obtaining water from wells or by purchase from the railroad. In 1918, a municipal electrical power plant began operation. That same year, voters approved school-district plans to construct a new four-room building. Until then, the district had been able to accommodate the area's small student population in the two-room Wickenburg Grammar School, later supplemented by a two-room frame-and-tent addition. But now enrollment was increasing—it reached 130 in 1920—and the teaching staff had grown to four. Furthermore, the district needed more space for its "advanced class," which it now offered in addition to its primary and intermediate classes and which served as the first two years of high school for many of Wickenburg's children. When the new building, which cost $23,000 to build and furnish, was opened in 1920, the district's budget of $7,155 was more than seven times what it had been in 1908.

Despite these changes, though, the perception of Wickenburg as a mining town persisted. Describing Wickenburg in his book *Arizona the Wonderland*, George Wharton James wrote in 1917: "While there are a number of ranches up and down the river, where the ranchers avail themselves of the rich bottom lands of the canyon, the greatest assets of the town and the district in which it lies are its wonderful climate and the mineral riches of the surrounding mountains." Thirty years later, recalling his years as principal of the town's school in the late 1910s, W. T. Machan offered a similar assessment of the town's character: "The town was [a] typical mining town with all the landmarks of a typical mining town, even to the principal being a good poker player and exercising his art in the speakeasies of the town. . . . The community consisted of miners and cowboys who always made life very interesting."

The Beginnings of a Ranching Economy

Through all of these changes, there remained one constant: the small community of families, both Anglo and Mexican American, who earned their livings by adapting to the shifting labor market. When jobs were available, they worked for local mining companies, often attempting to develop their own claims as well. At other times, they took whatever wage labor jobs were available, working for local businesses or for the railroad. Those with fewer skills or who were new to the area often worked as laborers, especially when the railroad was building nearby. Almost everyone had some kind of garden, and many people raised chickens or kept a horse or cow. Those who possessed enough land and water further supplemented their cash incomes with farming and small-scale livestock raising.

However, only those residents with access to the river and its ribbon of good soil could make farming and ranching anything approaching a full-time activity. Elsewhere, would-be ranchers and farmers found themselves lacking sufficient grass and water to raise large numbers of livestock, let alone to grow crops. Those who settled on desert land away from the river often found life difficult and prosperity elusive. Describing her childhood in Aguila, about twenty-five miles west of Wickenburg, Hazel Matchette recalled that her family's only source of water was the tank belonging to the railroad. Paying 50 cents per barrel, Hazel and her siblings carried the water to their house by burro, often making several trips a day during the summer. "We had no fresh meat, no ice, no fresh milk, nothing of the comforts of life," she later said. "There was a store in town [but] he didn't carry much; once in a while he would have some food. When my Dad came he would bring meat and things but no milk."

Still, despite less than ideal conditions, the farming and ranching economy of Wickenburg and the surrounding area began to show signs of real growth after 1900. Over the next decade, the number of persons who claimed agricultural occupations rose dramatically, from only fifteen persons in 1900 to ninety-two persons in 1910. The most significant change was in ranching; while only one Wickenburg resident described himself as a rancher to the 1900 census-takers, fifty-three persons did so in 1910.

In part, this reflected the pressures that population growth elsewhere in Arizona put on those seeking to make a living from the land; with the best land and water sources already claimed, new arrivals and new generations had to seek out acreage previously considered marginal. (This, more than anything else, explains the availability of homestead land in Arizona well into the 1930s.) It also was due to the railroad, which helped make stock raising more economically feasible by lowering the cost of transportation. Rather than drive their livestock to Ash Fork for shipping, which took time and reduced the sale weight of livestock, Wickenburg ranchers could now ship directly from town. As for the specific nature of the livestock business in and around Wickenburg, it appears that during the earliest decades of this century, sheep and goats were more plentiful than cattle. While the former could sustain themselves on the sparsely vegetated hillsides, the latter were confined largely to the Hassayampa River bottom and other well-watered areas.

A "Progressive" Town

The time when Wickenburg could truly call itself a ranching community was still in the future and would not come until the 1920s and 1930s. For now, mining and ranching coexisted as the economic supports of the community, and it was anyone's guess which would prove the most important in the long run.

Although Wickenburg's population declined slightly between 1910 and 1920, the town had grown and developed to such an extent that it was fundamentally different from the small mining community that Henry Wickenburg had presided over for many years. When George

Wharton James, a noted travel writer, visited the town in the mid-1910s, he had nothing but praise for Wickenburg—a striking contrast to many earlier travelers who criticized the town's dining and lodging facilities and noted its residents' apparent lack of energy. "It is a live town and its people are progressive," he wrote. "Its well-graded streets, pleasant homes and well-furnished stores make it a desirable residence spot."

Furthermore, James observed, Wickenburg had "most of the attributes of the larger cities, with a happy freedom from the undesirable features." Most significantly, James praised the town's climate. "There are many hundreds of people scattered over the world to-day who are enjoying life fully restored by a remedial sojourn in its pure, dry atmosphere," he claimed. Even if he was exaggerating a little—the town's guest ranch and tourist industries did not yet exist—James had identified what would turn out to be Wickenburg's greatest economic asset and the source of virtually all its future growth.

View of Wickenburg looking east toward Tegner Street
and St. Anthony of Padua Catholic Church, 1916.

A wagon parked in front of Brayton Commercial Company, circa 1910. Among the men standing at the right are Ramón Valencia (second from right) and Ygnacio Garcia (right).

Schoolchildren in front of the Wickenburg Grammar School (later renamed the Garcia School), circa 1916. Those identified are Mary O'Brien (left), Francisca Ocampo (second from left), and Eva Ocampo (fifth from left), in the back row; and Marcella Ocampo (third from left) and Anthony "Tony" O'Brien (fourth from left), in the front row.

(Above) The Vernetta Hotel, established in 1905 by Elizabeth Smith, for many years was Wickenburg's best hotel.

(Opposite, top) Brayton Commercial Company, which opened in 1906, for many years was Wickenburg's largest store. It later was the first home of the Desert Caballeros Western Museum.

(Left) Menno Yaggy and his Modern Dairy delivery wagon, circa 1915.

Monte Cristo mine, circa 1910.

(*Opposite, top*) Alvin Purdy and the Monarch Mining and Smelting Company truck, circa 1912.

(*Right*) Crossing the Hassayampa River, circa 1916.

View of Railroad Street (now Frontier Street) looking northwest, 1915.

The first automobile hearse used in Wickenburg; the driver is not identified.

Charles Hyder (left) and three unidentified men in his automobile garage on Tegner Street, circa 1920.

Floyd Tom Kellis in front of his bakery on Railroad Street
(now Frontier Street), sometime in the 1920s.

Party of unidentified motorists in front of the Baxter
Hotel on Center Street, circa 1920.

5 The Dude Ranch Capital of the World

TO TRAVELERS PASSING THROUGH Wickenburg in the early 1920s, the town must have seemed an unlikely candidate for a tourist center. It had no paved streets or sidewalks—the more prosperous businesses built their own boardwalks—and there was only one bank (newly opened), a handful of small restaurants, and one substantial hotel. The quiet streets of the "dusty, little town"—as one new arrival described Wickenburg—were frequented by miners, cowboys, and sheep herders, and visitors were as likely to hear Spanish spoken as they were English.

Occasionally automobile tourists from Los Angeles, Phoenix, and Tucson passed through town, and railroad passengers on the Santa Fe Railroad continued to alight for meals at the Vernetta Hotel. However, most tourists in the West were wealthy easterners and midwesterners whose standards of accommodation and service were not likely to be met in a town as small as Wickenburg. When they did travel to Arizona for their vacations, it was to such establishments as the Castle Hot Springs, a luxury resort situated east of Wickenburg on the southern slopes of the Bradshaw Mountains.

In the end, though, these handicaps proved to be ephemeral. After all, Wickenburg had a matchless winter climate, excellent railroad connections, and a prime location on the new national highway to the West Coast. As the number of tourists visiting the West steadily increased, and as more of them came searching for an authentically "western" experience, Wickenburg was ideally situated to offer them a new kind of travel accommodation: the dude ranch or, as it is called nowadays, guest ranch. In a little more than a decade, the erstwhile mining town was advertising itself as the "dude ranch capital of the world."

Early Tourist Establishments

For nearly two decades, Castle Hot Springs was the only tourist business in the Wickenburg area. Purchased in the late 1880s by a group headed by Prescott businessman Frank Murphy, and opened as a resort in 1896, Castle Hot Springs catered to wealthy tourists who demanded privacy and first-class accommodations. Guests typically arrived by train and were met at the resort's own depot, Hot Springs Junction, by a coach (later an automobile) that took them and their luggage to the mountain retreat. Once there, they indulged in such activities as tennis and horseback riding, and they took frequent baths in the warm-water springs, which were supposed to have restorative and medicinal properties. Of course, the main attraction at Castle Hot Springs was Arizona's warm winter climate. "It would seem impossible to claim too much for this favored spot," a publicity brochure from the early 1900s stated. "The mountain climate, mild and balmy, is extremely conducive to good sleep. The quiet restfulness brings relaxation and refreshment to body, soul and spirit."

Because it was located well to the east of town and had its own railroad depot, Castle Hot Springs had little direct impact on Wickenburg. Occasionally guests would travel to Wickenburg to watch a rodeo, but generally they had no need to visit the town. It was not until 1912, when the Garden of Allah was established just south of town on the banks of the Hassayampa River, that Wickenburg finally acquired its own tourist "resort." The Garden of Allah was the brainchild of a retired New York physician and his wife, John and Frances Sanger, who purchased the riverside farm developed by Frederick Brill, one of the first Anglo settlers in Wickenburg. Taking advantage of natural springs that fed several ponds and kept the Hassayampa River flowing year-round through the farm, the Sangers advertised their resort as an "oasis in the desert" and touted its appeal to the "hunter, pleasure seeker, tired business man and convalescent."

The Garden of Allah offered rather rustic accommodations compared to Castle Hot Springs; guests were housed in simple cabins with screened porches. Meals featuring fresh milk, butter, eggs, and chickens raised on the premises were served in the original adobe Brill farmhouse "by the best of Japanese servants," and guests were assured that "all the privacy of home is combined with the pleasures of outdoor western life and the conveniences of hotel service." Although the Garden of Allah was intended as a year-round resort, it appears to have been most popular as a summer retreat for Phoenix residents. Easily reached by train or automobile, the resort offered a quick escape from the Salt River Valley's stifling summer heat. In many respects, the Garden of Allah was Wickenburg's first guest ranch, for it offered all the ingredients that would later make guest ranching in Wickenburg so popular: wholesome food, a relaxed atmosphere, outdoor activities such as horseback riding, and Arizona's warm winter climate.

Mining in the 1920s

The Garden of Allah remained a solitary venture for more than a decade, perhaps because its springs and lush riparian vegetation gave it an appeal that could not be duplicated elsewhere along the Hassayampa's normally dry banks. More important, perhaps, was the conviction of business owners and residents in Wickenburg that mining and ranching would continue to drive the town's future development. The town's newspaper, now called the *Miner,* proclaimed Wickenburg the "mining capital" of Arizona and devoted most of its editorial space to news of local mineral discoveries. However, though the *Miner* regularly reported new mineral "finds," from time to time asserting that one or the other would prove to be the largest ever in the district, its editor never was able to report that a local mine was beginning regular production. An example of this phenomenon is provided by the Monte Cristo, a silver mine that was reputed to be one of the more valuable properties in the state. After several years of reporting improvements at the mine that included electrification and surveying for a railroad spur line, the *Miner* advised its readers that despite seventeen years of development work, it "never has been the policy of the management to ship out ore."

The *Miner* editor's claims to the contrary, the local mining economy was struggling. As had been the case for a number of years, Wickenburg benefited from its surrounding mines only because investors—most of them from outside the state—continued to pour money into local mining prospects. The Octave mine was worked fitfully between 1918 and 1922, then closed for six years. Beginning in 1928, its owners had some luck extracting gold and silver using the flotation process, but in 1930, operations were suspended again; soon most of the mine workings were flooded. At the Congress, once the most productive gold mine in the area, the outlook was even less promising: by 1920, the surface equipment and four-mile spur railroad line to the mine had been dismantled. For the remainder of the decade and into the 1930s, various lessees processed ore from the mine's dumps using the cyanide process, but none was able to sustain production for any length of time. Attempts were even made to reopen the Vulture in 1927, but they never amounted to more than preliminary development work.

As for the Monte Cristo, it never quite lived up to its promise. After pouring thousands into the silver mine's development, owner C. C. Julian was reported to have earned only fifteen thousand dollars in profits. Whether he was really interested in developing the mine for long-term production is a matter of some dispute. Soon after he bought the mine from Phoenix businessman Ezra Thayer, Julian combined it with other mine holdings and began selling shares in the Julian Merger Mines. When securities officials in California halted sale of the stock because of problems stemming from deceptive oil stock promotions that Julian had earlier advertised, he simply reincorporated the company as the Monte Cristo Mining Company and kept selling. Late in 1927, a group of Arizona shareholders filed suit, claiming that the company was a fraudulent enterprise and that Julian had failed to properly develop the Monte Cristo property, allowing its workings to become flooded. The plaintiffs won, but their victory came too late to keep the mine in production.

Ranching in the 1920s

Mining promotions to the contrary, the economic pendulum in Wickenburg had definitely swung toward ranching, which now was the mainstay of the area's economy. Thousands of sheep and goats roamed the hillsides and desert expanses around Wickenburg, while cattle grazed up and down the Hassayampa River bottom. Fueled by a booming market for mohair, goats were perhaps the most profitable animals for local ranchers. At each of the two annual shearing seasons, an estimated twenty-five thousand dollars came into the town—a substantial sum in the early 1920s.

On the basis of numbers alone, though, sheep were the dominant animal in the vicinity of Wickenburg, a fact that did not sit well with some of the local cattle ranchers. "It wasn't exactly a war," Pete Fletcher recalled many years later, "but the cattlemen claimed that the sheep herders were keeping their sheep in one place too long and pulling up the grass by the roots and destroying future growth so the cattle wouldn't get enough feed. Actually it was the climate which started drying up about that time." Some cattle ranchers blamed sheep for the "barren" appearance of the hills surrounding town, while others claimed that cattle would not drink from water sources frequented by sheep. Furthermore, the divide between cattle and sheep ranchers was cultural and linguistic, for most of the sheep herders were Basques or Mexicans who preferred their native languages. Over time, though, the tension between the two groups dissipated as more local ranchers began raising both cattle and sheep.

The impact of ranching on Wickenburg was more than economic; it also shaped the town's character. Because most of the local cattle grazed along the river, where the grass was thickest, roundup time inevitably brought cattle into the town's center. Describing the scene to an interviewer, Fletcher said, "One group of cowboys and wranglers would go up the river, and another group would go down. They would round up all the cattle and bring them in where the bridge is now. They would go up the main street, which was all dirt then. Clouds of dust flew. The shopkeepers would close their shops and come out with broomsticks and help herd the cattle, all the way up to the depot." Residents also had to cope with strays that wandered out of the riverbed to graze in town. To deal with this problem, town officials authorized the marshal to impound strays, which were released to their owners only after payment of a fine. "At the rate which stock rushes thru town to get the savory grasses growing around the streets and empty lots," the *Arizona State Miner* editorialized in 1920, "it looks like the city pound may have to be enlarged to cover at least a couple of acres."

Sheep ranching had its own rhythms, as well, most of them reflecting the migratory patterns followed by herders searching for good grass. Many sheep-raising operations maintained winter quarters in the Wickenburg area and then moved in the summer to communities such as Ash Fork or Williams. Recalling her family's seasonal moves, Aimee Pouquette Simpson said, "When we moved back and forth we moved everything: the chickens, horses, six kids, my mother, and we had a great big iron wood stove in the kitchen that we moved, too. We loaded up the car and pickups and moved it all." Meanwhile, the herders would walk or ride with the sheep as they made their way slowly up into the cool northern country. A herder's life was a lonely one, and the pay was low—typically thirty dollars per month, plus shelter (generally a tent) and food, in the 1920s and early 1930s. As the countryside around Wickenburg became more developed, the long drives were gradually abandoned. "After a time we couldn't trail the sheep any more because fences cut off the trail, so we railed them and later trucked," Simpson told an interviewer many years later.

As was the case in most other Arizona communities, Wickenburg's desert environment imposed limits on local ranchers. Located in the lower Sonoran Desert, Wickenburg was more arid and had less forage than other ranching areas in Arizona. Consequently, the most profitable outfits belonged to longtime ranchers whose spreads gave them access to the Hassayampa River, where their cattle could find water and grass most of the year. Ranchers located away from the riverbed were forced to rely on groundwater pumped from wells, which could be quite expensive to dig and maintain depending on the depth of the water table, and on large amounts of costly supplemental feed.

Confronted with these facts of desert life, Wickenburg residents continued to hope that some way might be found to construct a reservoir on the Hassayampa River. In 1920, it looked like they would get their wish when Joseph Wittman, a New York capitalist, proposed building a new dam at the site of the collapsed Walnut Grove Dam. Four years later, the state land commissioner gave Wittman (the son-in-law of the builder of the original Walnut Grove Dam) permission to undertake the project. However, Wittman's plans soon foundered on the obstacles that had always plagued Arizona reclamationists: high costs and opposition from landowners and water right holders along the Hassayampa River. The Nadaburg Irrigation District in particular opposed the project, and its members' refusal to allow the reservoir to be built on their land eventually led to the project's demise.

Wickenburg's First Guest Ranches

As it turns out, ranching proved to be Wickenburg's economic salvation in ways that no one could have anticipated in the early 1900s. During the early 1920s, both rainfall and cattle prices dropped sharply across Arizona, forcing ranchers to reduce the size of their herds or, in more than a few cases, go out of business altogether. Confronted with this bitter prospect, a handful of local ranchers turned to tourists for extra money—just as many earlier ranchers had supplemented their earnings with outside income from mining and wage labor. Some developed their own guest ranches, while others rented their property to newcomers who had enough capital to develop a new business. "It was a turning point in Wickenburg between cattle ranching and mining and dude ranching," recalled Anthony "Tony" O'Brien, whose family leased its ranch to the developers of the Remuda Ranch,

Wickenburg's first full-time guest ranch. "There was very little money in circulation and dude ranching was the only money. Like in mining, [they] had to go out there [East] to get the money; but in dude ranching, they brought the money here."

Looking back on this pivotal decade many years later, another long-time ranch owner, Sophie Burden, suggested that the guest ranches "brought new money and new life to the town" at a time when drought and low cattle prices were leading some residents to predict that Wickenburg would soon resemble the town of the late 1870s, when it nearly became a ghost town. Not only did the guest ranches attract tourists who stayed for weeks (and sometimes months), spending money on food, western clothing, and sundry goods; they also attracted new residents with investment capital. From the beginning of its development, the guest ranch industry in Wickenburg was dependent on outside investors—often persons who had first visited the town as tourists themselves. In fact, of the first guest ranches in the 1920s, only a small minority were started by local ranchers.

The timing could not have been better for Wickenburg, for changes in the tourist industry that would help create a market for guest ranches were just getting underway in the 1920s. Until the arrival of the automobile gave vacationers the freedom to travel on their own, most tourists went to large resorts, many of which had been built by railroads. Catering to well-to-do travelers (who made up most of the tourist population during the early decades of this century), these resorts emphasized decorum and proper social relations; for example, changing clothes several times a day and "dressing for dinner" were not uncommon resort practices. However, this sense of propriety was at odds with the increasing informality of American life. And as more middle- and upper-class Americans took up vigorous outdoor activities, the languorous style of the traditional resorts—where the main activities were sitting on porches, strolling, and socializing—seemed increasingly out-of-date.

At the same time, attitudes toward the American West were changing. As industrialization and urbanization accelerated in the United States, and as Americans began to feel estranged from their frontier past, interest in the American West as a remnant of the frontier began to grow. Because Arizona had experienced much less development than other states, even other western states, it offered travelers a chance to rediscover "untamed nature" and the primitive, rustic conditions of the frontier. In Arizona, tourists could relax, "be themselves," and live a more "authentic" existence away from the pressures and demands of urban life.

Guest ranches—dude ranches, as they were commonly called during the early years of the trade—were the perfect accommodation for tourists who wanted to experience the "real" West. Guest ranches were the antithesis of hotels and traditional resorts. Most were run by their owners, who treated clients as "guests" in their homes. The ranches emphasized informality and familiarity, encouraged visitors to wear casual western clothing and address each other (and the owner) by first name, and allowed guests to engage in ranch activities as they saw fit, without following a schedule. Most importantly, they advertised a western lifestyle that combined outdoor activities such as horseback riding and fishing with enjoyment of Arizona's winter climate and sunshine, unstructured relaxation, wholesome ranch food, proximity to nature, remoteness from urban development, and a studied informality.

In the Wickenburg area, the traditional type of resort had been represented since 1896 by Castle Hot Springs. Life at the springs was slow-paced and emphasized "less strenuous forms of exercise" (as a brochure put it in 1910), such as walking, tennis, automobile driving, shuffleboard, and riding on "gentle mountain ponies." Photographs in the resort's publicity literature show male guests in coats and ties and female guests in long skirts, corsets, and large hats—even when playing tennis. The Garden of Allah, though it was not a guest ranch in the way that term is understood today, represented something of a departure from the traditional resort. Its guests not only rode horses; they also met prospectors and even panned for gold in the Hassayampa River. The accommodations were more rustic than at Castle Hot Springs, as well.

The first guest ranch in Wickenburg was started by Leo Weaver, who rented the Bar F X Ranch from Tony O'Brien's family in 1923 or 1924 and began taking in guests who paid for their food and lodging (in both tents and cabins). If they desired, the guests also helped with ranch work. In 1925, Weaver lost his lease on the ranch and was forced to close. However, by then others were getting into the guest ranch business in Wickenburg. Romaine Lowdermilk, who had homesteaded a ranch called the Kay El Bar, was one of the few local ranchers to try running a guest ranch on his own; he began taking in guests at about the same time as Weaver. The Kay El Bar was primarily a working ranch; as Tony O'Brien later described it, as a guest ranch it was "an off-the-cuff type of thing and hadn't quite ranked to the term 'dude ranching' yet." In addition to Lowdermilk, two young men from the East, Jack Burden and Lewis C. "Bob" White, were trying their hands at guest ranching, having taken up the lease on the Bar F X in preparation for opening a new guest ranch, the Remuda.

The Remuda Ranch, which became one of the longest-running guest ranch operations in the Wickenburg area, opened in 1925 with an initial investment of two thousand dollars borrowed from Burden and White's families. The Remuda was a simple operation by today's guest ranch standards. Advertising "invigorating air with continuous sunshine throughout the winter" and "good food, appetizingly served," the ranch's first publicity pamphlet featured a stylish cover drawing of a cowboy atop a bucking bronco and promised guests "outdoor life on the range"—all for $35 per week, plus $10 per week for the unlimited use of a horse.

When Burden and White carried these brochures to the Phoenix Chamber of Commerce in the fall of 1925 to promote their new endeavor, they happened to meet a family inquiring about ranches where they could enjoy an extended stay. They persuaded the family to try the Remuda, but when asked when they could take their new guests, the two men allowed that they had not planned to open for another few days. Begging the family to wait for their "official" opening, Burden and White immediately went to stores in Phoenix and Wickenburg to purchase furniture, food, and equipment. "We went into the general store and opened up an account and everybody helped us and we were getting people faster than we could put up another building to take care of them," White later recalled. "Dude ranches were in demand."

After running the Remuda for one year as partners, the two men went their separate ways. White opened his own guest ranch, the Monte Vista (also called the M-Bar-V), on a hillside overlooking the town—the first guest ranch to be located away from the river—while Burden, with his new wife Sophie, continued to operate the Remuda. Two years later, in 1928, the Burdens left the Bar F X after a rent dispute, purchased land on the east side of the river, and began building a new Remuda Ranch from the ground up. Meanwhile, Leo Weaver had continued his guest ranch, by now called the Circle Flying W, at the former site of the Garden of Allah, which he leased at least through 1928. And Romaine Lowdermilk, after selling a half-interest in his property to Henry Warbasse in 1927, added several buildings to the Kay El Bar and established it as a full-time guest ranch. By the fall of 1927, when these four ranches were all in operation, the Wickenburg *Miner* was promoting the town as "the home of the dude ranches."

Guest Ranching in Wickenburg

Perhaps the most appealing feature of the guest ranches was their informality; except for meals and occasional group activities, guests were free to pursue their own interests. "No one feels he must participate in a planned program of activities," the Triangle W Ranch noted in a 1940s brochure. "[Our] guests relax and enjoy our 'do as you please' type of program." As part of this informality, the ranches encouraged their guests to wear western attire—denim pants, cowboy boots, broad-brimmed hats, and kerchiefs—for outdoor activities, and casual sports clothes the remainder of the time. "You wear what you want to wear," a Remuda brochure advised. "If you haven't visited the West before we would suggest that you wait and buy your clothes out here. You will see brightly colored shirts everywhere, but you won't see many men with coats on in the dining room." Many ranchers urged their patrons to buy their new western clothes at local stores, a practice that endeared the fledgling guest ranchers to local business owners.

The predominant activity at the guest ranches was horseback riding. Some ranches, such as the Kay El Bar and Monte Vista, allowed their patrons to herd and brand cattle and otherwise help with ranch chores. However, this practice gradually disappeared as fewer guest ranches carried on the activities of a working ranch and as fewer guests showed an interest in such labors. Most patrons preferred recreational riding, which they did either on their own or in groups under the tutelage of ranch wranglers. Ranches also conducted overnight pack trips and meal rides. These offered patrons the quintessential western meal, the cookout, where (in the words of a Bar F X brochure) "the cowboys cook the meals over the campfire—a meal that will tempt the most delicate of appetites—sizzling steaks, the aroma of coffee, the silvery moon for which Arizona is rapidly becoming famous, the strumming of guitars."

In addition to riding, other activities included hunting trips, fishing trips to the Colorado River and to mountain lakes across the state, and "motoring" excursions to such well-known tourist destinations as the Grand Canyon, Roosevelt Dam, and Casa Grande. Ranches also shuttled their guests into town, and occasionally into Phoenix, for shopping, movies, and dining. And there were cooperative events that brought all the ranches' patrons together for socializing and entertainment. The most frequent of these were the rodeos held at each ranch on a rotating basis, but they also included dances and parties, an annual horse show, the annual Cattle Rustlers Ball, and occasional events such as art shows.

From the beginning, the guest ranches took pains to distance themselves from actual ranches in terms of comfort and convenience. "All rooms, with or without hot and cold running water, are comfortably furnished and homelike," the Wickenburg *Miner* reminded readers in 1927. "The rancher's own dairy, poultry and fresh vegetables supply the table with a high grade of food served in an appetizing manner." Although ranches in the early years could dispense with such amenities as full private bathrooms with hot water, knowing that most of their guests expected the accommodations to be somewhat rustic, by the Second World War standards had risen to the point where guest ranches had become synonymous with understated luxury. "The 1944 model of dudes who come to Arizona to get wrangled want all the comforts of Fifth Avenue, while they 'rough it' and 'go western,'" a hospitality industry publication noted. "The "M-Bar-V" gives it to 'em. Bob [White] rolls 'em out to the ranch in his car. Deposits 'em in comfortable rooms that are equipped with electricity and hot air heat. Cottages have open fireplaces besides. Showers and baths for every room. Comfortable beds. Wonderful maid service."

All these activities took place in a "western" atmosphere that was artfully enhanced by the guest ranch owners. The Bar F X in the late 1930s promised its guests "western atmosphere, and with a little touch of the Indian in evidence." The Remuda Ranch, whose brochures stated that guests came to Wickenburg to satisfy "a deep-down yearning to lead a free and easy outdoor life," promised not only "peace and contentment" but also a magical encounter with the "old West" and its celebrated denizen, the cowboy. "Just the sky and the air and the earth underfoot is an adventure, and youth is in the saddle once more," a ranch brochure suggested. After hearing the wranglers' "strange, weird songs" and "rollicking jokes," guests would see cowboys in an entirely new light: "They are a vital part of the strange wild land you almost missed by living thirty years too late and many miles far too east."

Part of the ranches' western atmosphere—which would later be referred to as the "southwestern lifestyle"—was their emphasis on "family-style" living and congeniality. Guests, who were generally wealthy and thus able to afford long winter vacations, often came for the entire season. Those with children either brought their own tutors or placed their children in the classes that most ranches offered, generally under the supervision of a spouse or ranch employee hired for that purpose. Although only a few ranches had formal policies on the length of stay, none of the guest ranches catered to the transient trade and many refused overnight guests.

The long stays, combined with the tendency of many guests to return year after year, led guest ranch owners to regard their patrons as a sort of extended family. The Remuda, for example, published a newsletter that was sent to all its patrons during the off-season and contained news from guests of weddings, births, career changes, travel activities, and occasionally the decision to establish a winter home in Wickenburg. Because so many of the guests knew each other, most activities at the ranches were communal in nature; couples and families rarely did things on their own. The centerpiece of ranch social life was an evening spent around the fireplace in the ranch's main lodge or living room. At the Monte Vista, as described by a writer in the 1940s, Bob White held court with his guitar, singing cowboy songs to guests who chatted, played cards and checkers, and even gave performances of their own.

Although the guest ranches advertised in one way or another, most of their patrons came by referral, either from established guests or from friends of the ranch owner. Because their guests stayed for such long periods, ranch owners took pains to assure their compatibility and congeniality. This helped reinforce the family-style atmosphere at the ranches, but it also exacted a price: most ranches catered to a "restricted clientele" (in the words of the Remuda Ranch). What this meant in practice varied from ranch to ranch, and over time. In the early years, the 1920s and 1930s, ranches took pains to distance themselves from sanatoria, refusing to accept guests with tuberculosis or other communicable diseases. But the restrictions also were racial and ethnic; for example, "restricted clientele" often meant that Jews were not welcome—a sentiment made explicit by the Bar F X, which in the 1930s was "maintained for the patronage of gentile guests." By requiring references of every guest, the ranches were in a position to refuse any person whose presence would violate the norms of segregation that prevailed in the travel industry virtually everywhere in the country.

Town Life

Looking back on this period from the vantage point of the present, it is difficult to precisely gauge the impact of the guest ranches on the town. Certainly they affected the ambiance of Wickenburg, as wealthy tourists began showing up on sightseeing and shopping trips, occasionally patronizing the saloons and cafes or attending local dances. More importantly, the ranches brought much-needed business. Wickenburg's population, after stagnating for several years, started to climb again in the late 1920s, probably in response to economic growth stimulated by highway improvements and the development of the guest ranches. By 1930, 734 persons lived in the town—an increase of more than two hundred since the previous census in 1920. Just two years before, in 1928, the recently established Wickenburg High School District had opened its first school, an impressive building situated on a five-acre tract of land donated by the family of Francis X. O'Brien, who established the Bar F X Ranch.

But in most respects, Wickenburg remained largely unaffected by the outside world's newfound interest in the Southwest's climate and scenery; except for the ranch guests, who were relatively few in number, not many tourists passed through town in the 1920s and into the Depression. As a result, Wickenburg continued much as it always had, a community attuned to the rhythms of rural life. Most activities in town ended at 10 o'clock at night, thanks to a municipal power plant that was too small to provide around-the-clock service. During the summertime, many residents spent as much time as possible—including sleeping—outside to avoid the stifling heat inside their uncooled and often poorly insulated homes. Whether Anglo or Mexican American, Wickenburg residents gathered under porches and ramadas to eat, drink, socialize, and entertain themselves with music and dancing in a setting that kept neighbors in regular contact with each other.

And despite the emergence of its fledgling tourist industry, Wickenburg's economy still depended to a large extent on the commerce its merchants and business owners carried on with local ranchers, cowboys, mine owners, and miners. Its streets shaded by mulberry trees and its downtown served by a full complement of stores, restaurants, and lodging houses, Wickenburg must have seemed like an oasis to ranchers and miners who lived in the surrounding desert and mountains. "Every Friday, they would come into town and about drop their whole paycheck," longtime resident Aimee Pouquette Simpson recalled. "They would stay in town for the weekend and buy groceries for the week. They are the ones who really helped the town."

For the most part, Wickenburg residents still conducted their business in the stores and other establishments lining Railroad Street (now Frontier Street); the Belmont Hotel (formerly the Vernetta), Brayton Commercial Company's general store, and the post office were here, as were several boarding houses, a drugstore, eating places, and other shops. When the town had a bank—a service it lacked in the mid-1930s—it, too, was located on Railroad Street. But as the town grew and as automobile traffic through Wickenburg gradually increased, businesses began to migrate to Tegner and Center streets. By 1931, four automobile-related firms, two of them large garages, were located in a two-block stretch of Tegner from its intersection with Center Street (now Wickenburg Way) to just past First Street (now Apache). Across the street, a new Pay'n Takit store—part of a chain operated by the predecessor to today's Safeway—had been opened. And just down the street, at Tegner and Second (now Yavapai), an auto camp greeted travelers entering town from the north.

When commercial amusements began to appear in town, they were simple affairs. In the mid-1920s, William Bass, who earlier had developed a tourist camp at the Grand Canyon, built a swimming pool just across the river from town. For 15 cents a person, residents could cool off with a dip in the concrete pool, which at night was illuminated by lights strung in nearby trees. Within a few years, the town also had its first golf course, a rustic and grassless nine holes scraped out of the desert just north of town. Recalling a turn on the course in the late 1920s, Tony O'Brien described the first hole as one of many challenges that awaited local golfers: "[we would] tee off in a whole bunch of cactus in a little clear spot, over the cactus onto a little flat where the Indians had camped because you could find pottery lying around."

In addition to the swimming pool, Bass also built a campground and gas station on his riverside property. Later his son Bill, who took over the property's management, added an outdoor dance pavilion. Bass Pavilion, as it was first called, consisted of a maple floor resting on rubber blocks, a frame roof, and open sides draped with canvas that could be raised in hot weather to let in the cool nighttime breezes. It also doubled as a roller-skating rink, and the first movies in Wickenburg were shown at the pavilion. At some point, the pavilion acquired the name El Recreo, and for years it was the main facility in town capable of accommodating a large event. Even the guest ranches used El Recreo. "We had it fixed up real nice with booths and each dude ranch had a private booth there and would bring their guests to the dance at night," the younger Bass later recalled. "We always saw to it that the wranglers at the ranch had a couple of hundred tickets so he'd bring all of his guests to the dances. We usually had a pretty good orchestra [and] played western music."

Unfortunately, not all Wickenburg residents were welcome at some of these recreational facilities. As in most Arizona towns, Mexican Americans were barred from swimming at the Bass pool. Instead, they swam at a gravel pit on the Hassayampa River that was deep enough to hold water year-round. Whether El Recreo was formally segregated is unclear, but it would have been highly unusual, given the racial attitudes that prevailed at the time, for Anglos and Mexican Americans to mingle at a private dance. During these years, the Mexican-American community generally held its own dances and social events, gathering at the Garcia dance hall (located in the 1920s near Center Street), the Baxter Opera House (at Center and Tegner streets), or in private homes.

Development of Local Highways

One of the major reasons that Wickenburg's early tourist development was confined to the guest ranches was that its highway connections to the rest of the state, let alone the rest of the country, remained poor well into the 1920s. While other communities in the state were finding ways to benefit from the automobile's new popularity, and with it a growing stream of Americans taking vacations in their cars,

Wickenburg was severely hampered by the lack of a reliable bridge across the Hassayampa River. Until 1914, when the first bridge across the riverbed was built by the county, drivers had to ford the river—if they could cross at all. Only two years after the concrete structure was built, one of its spans was washed out by flooding, and the town again had no bridge until a new one was built in 1920–21. Even the new bridge, constructed of steel and concrete, was not immune to damage; one of its approaches washed out in the winter of 1927.

The construction of the second Hassayampa bridge was one of several projects that inaugurated a period of intense road-building in the 1920s as Arizona, stimulated by new federal highway legislation, began to improve its roads and integrate them into the evolving national highway system. Wickenburg was luckier than most Arizona communities when it came time for the highway department to select the routes for the state's new federal highways. Not only was the Phoenix-Prescott road designated as part of Arizona's main north-south highway (US 89); the Phoenix-Ehrenberg road also was included, as part of the main transcontinental highway across the southern United States (US 60). Originally, state engineers wanted the north-south highway to run through the Black Canyon, along the route now followed by I-17, but pressure from Yavapai County—which had just passed a highway bond issue to finance improvements on the existing road—persuaded them to accept the Prescott-Wickenburg-Phoenix alignment instead. Thus, in 1922, Wickenburg found itself astride the intersection of two major highways, one of which (US 60) would carry all of the automobile and truck traffic between central Arizona and the West Coast.

Inclusion in the federal highway system did not bring immediate benefits, however, for the quality of the roads still left much to be desired. By 1925, the road from Phoenix to Wickenburg was only half paved; of the remaining half, part was "improved" gravel and the rest consisted of dirt stretches that were prone to flooding and washouts. The road north to Prescott was in even worse condition; though it was improved as far as Congress Junction, the remainder was not even in the state road system and was officially classified as "rough."

As for the highway westward to California, it was merely a county dirt road not yet incorporated into the state system.

Although the state legislature was reluctant to fund new roads, its parsimony was more than offset by the actions of Congress, which increased federal highway appropriations during the 1930s as a way of stimulating the economy. As a result, much of Arizona's modern highway system was built during the Depression. By 1931, the highway from Phoenix to Wickenburg was paved as far as Morristown; two years later, in 1933, the pavement reached Wickenburg. Progress on US 60 from Wickenburg to Ehrenberg was even more rapid. In 1931, the road was improved dirt from Wickenburg to Salome, unimproved dirt from Salome to Quartzsite, and improved gravel from there to the border. By the end of 1932, the Quartzsite-Ehrenberg section was paved and all but a short stretch of the remainder had been converted to improved gravel. A year later, all but a short segment between Wickenburg and Salome was paved, and that was completed by October 1934. Construction on US 89 north to Prescott and the Grand Canyon proceeded at a similarly rapid pace. By the end of 1933, the road was paved to Congress Junction. A year later, all of the highway between Ash Fork and Wickenburg was paved except the White Spar Highway, which was still being built. Construction on that final, mountainous segment was completed in January 1935.

The Depression

From the perspective of motorists, the improvements brought by the road construction binge were tangible; now, for example, it was possible to make the trip from Phoenix to Los Angeles in only twelve hours by automobile. But for towns along the roads, like Wickenburg, the benefits of the new system were much slower in coming, largely because the Depression kept middle-class automobile tourists at home.

As it was for many other communities in Arizona, the Depression was a mixed experience for Wickenburg and its residents. Despite the collapse of the stock market, most of the wealthy in the nation continued to do quite well; consequently, few interrupted their seasonal migrations to the Wickenburg area, and the guest ranches suffered only a slight decline in their business during the 1930s. "We really didn't feel the Depression until about 1933," Remuda Ranch operator Sophie Burden later remembered. In fact, the number of guest ranches in the Wickenburg area remained stable during the 1930s, so that by 1938, there were seven ranches operating: the Bar F X, Lazy R C (formerly the Circle Flying W), Remuda, Monte Vista, Kay El Bar, Sombrero (located north of town), and Triangle W (to the west of town).

For those residents of Wickenburg who managed to keep their jobs and businesses, the Depression was often little more than an inconvenience; after all, most prices dropped during the early 1930s, a development that had the effect of raising the standard of living of anyone with an income. Still, certain groups—retail store owners, mine owners and miners, and unskilled laborers, to name a few—suffered grievously. Reflecting the downturn in prices and local trade, the Traders' Bank, by now the town's only such institution, was forced to close in 1933, leaving Wickenburg without a bank for the first time in years. The decline in employment and wages was especially painful for those Wickenburg residents who had gotten along in previous years by combining small-scale ranching and farming with whatever jobs, skilled or unskilled, were locally available. One such vulnerable resident, Ray Villa, had worked as a goat herder (for twenty dollars a month), a construction worker, and a miner before the Depression left him unemployed. "It was hard," Villa recalled many years later. "We used to go to the farms and steal corn. We killed a deer to eat and it was out of season."

Other area residents fought unemployment by taking to the hills and washes in search of gold, a venture in which they were joined by hundreds of unemployed men and families from the rest of the state and from across the country as well. One day's work might turn up only one-tenth of an ounce of gold, but the proceeds from that (about $3.50) were sufficient to keep a family from starving. Virtually every placer deposit in the state was reworked during the Depression by impoverished miners. Viewing the phenomenon from Prescott, the director of that city's Chamber of Commerce, Grace Sparkes, wrote to a friend: "Now that it is warmer they [the unemployed] are spreading out into the hills and mountains in the hope of placer mining and getting a few cents a day out of the gravel-bars that were worked fifty years ago. Sometimes they really do pan out a few cents—or once in a while get a dollar or more—but the old diggings are very lean of gold—having been worked over and over all these years."

Impoverished placer miners were not the only ones to learn, yet again, that the mines around Wickenburg had seen better days. Seeking to capitalize on the high price of gold, which was fixed at $35 an ounce, mining promoters worked to develop new properties and re-open older ones. Some of these failed, while others succeeded—at least for a time. In many respects, the Depression was the last fling for the town's mining economy. The Hassayampa Placer Gold Company gained control of ten sections of land along the river south of town and announced ambitious plans to dredge the riverbed for gold. However, for reasons that remain unclear, the company never carried out its plans. Developers at the old Congress Mine had better luck. In 1938, the same year the Congress post office was closed, a new 300-ton cyanide plant was installed at the mine. Its owners succeeded in re-processing the ore dumps and tailings left by previous operators until the mine was closed during the Second World War. Similar work was carried out near Yarnell by the Winslow Gold Mining Company in the late 1930s. Even the Vulture managed to see some new activity. The United Verde Extension Company, which had developed some of Jerome's copper mines, briefly carried out exploration work at the Vulture in 1930-31. The firm declined to begin full-scale production, but small-time operators were able to rework the ore dumps for a few years using a ten-stamp mill and the cyanide process.

Other local mines continued to operate, but it was often a hand-to-mouth existence. Roy Coxwell, whose family operated a cafe and later a tourist court in Wickenburg during the Depression, recalled how the owners of the Oro Grande Mine paid their workers: "Things were pretty tough around Wickenburg in those days, and the promoters that were promoting the mine weren't able to sell any stock, but they would issue the workers mine stock, and Mother had made a deal with old Dad Richards up at the Brayton Commercial Company to accept that stock for groceries, so that's kind of how they kept going in those lean years around Wickenburg. Of course, the guy that got stuck with all the stock when the thing finally closed was Dad Richards."

Ironically, the Depression brought some tangible benefits to Wickenburg in the form of government programs. Indeed, much of the town's modern infrastructure—its sidewalks and streets—dates from the 1930s, when the federal government sought to stimulate employment by distributing money to state and local governments for construction projects. Many of the town's first paved sidewalks and curbs were built by men hired under the Works Progress Administration (WPA), which also contributed funds for the construction of a new underpass on US 60 (replacing the old ground-level railroad crossing) and a new steel and concrete bridge across the Hassayampa River—both of which were completed in 1937.

Wickenburg's schools especially benefited from federal spending. At first, the Depression brought nothing but pain for the local school district; in 1933, after losing some of its state aid and seeing its property tax revenues fall, the school board cut its budget by 16 percent and asked teachers to forgo one-half month's salary. But in 1934, the district received a much-needed boost when the Civil Works Administration, the WPA's predecessor, provided funds for a new football stadium. That same year, the district received a federal government loan to help pay for a combined gymnasium and community building, which was completed in 1935. In 1936, the WPA financed several improvements to the elementary school. And three years later, in 1939, the district opened a new high school library paid for with a combination of WPA funds, state money, and local funds.

On the Threshold of Change

As the 1930s drew to a close, Wickenburg found itself poised on the threshold of change. Once a small, relatively isolated ranching and mining community, the town still depended to a great extent on these traditional industries not only for its livelihood but for its cultural identity. Yet Wickenburg, the self-proclaimed "Dude Ranch Capital of the World," also was becoming known to travelers around the world for its desert climate. Once the Depression ended, this reputation as a resort center was certain to bring not only tourists but also investors and new residents. Already Wickenburg's streets offered scenes that epitomized both the old and the new in Arizona. "Here cowboys and hard-rock miners rub shoulders with visitors from the neighboring guest ranches, which attract many internationally noted personages who go to Wickenburg to 'be themselves,'" a reporter for the *Arizona Republic* wrote after visiting the town in 1938. One of these prominent visitors was the English author J. B. Priestley, who did the town the favor of describing its winter climate as "one of the best in the world" in a 1937 article in *Harper's Magazine* and then in an autobiographical book called *Midnight on the Desert*, part of which was set at the Remuda Ranch.

The gradual transformation of Wickenburg into a tourist center was not an unwelcome change; the town's business community, led by the Round-Up Club (otherwise known as the Chamber of Commerce), worked hard to advertise the region's climate and friendly small-town atmosphere. Since the early 1920s, the town's businesses had sponsored a rodeo that served not only to entertain local ranch hands and families, but also to advertise Wickenburg and its guest ranches to residents of Phoenix, Tucson, and California. By the late 1930s, the rodeo had been incorporated into the Gold Rush Days, a multi-day festival that celebrated not only Wickenburg's ranching heritage but also its mining past. At the 1941 gathering, during which a monument to Henry Wickenburg was dedicated, miners (and would-be miners) matched their skills in burro loading, rock drilling, dry washing, and gold panning competitions.

But on the eve of the Second World War, this transformation was still in its earliest stages. Although well-established as a "junction community" (to use the words of one newspaper reporter), owing to the presence of US highways 60 and 89, Wickenburg's tourist economy was rather primitive by postwar standards. Except for the guest ranches, which never attracted large numbers of people and at any rate were not affordable for middle-class travelers, the only facilities catering to tourists were a few auto camps and gasoline stations. But this was likely to change, as Priestley had predicted in 1937. "I prophesy that as transport becomes quicker, cheaper, easier, the Wickenburg district will become increasingly important, for a winter climate as good as this will prove a better gold-mine than the Old Vulture, which Henry Wickenburg discovered while chasing his burro, ever was," he wrote. What no one, not even Priestley, could have foreseen in the late 1930s was that Wickenburg would be almost completely reshaped by the explosion in automobile travel and residential mobility that followed the Second World War.

Wickenburg baseball team, circa 1921. Those pictured are
Al E. Everts, the manager (in front), and (from left to
right) Peachy Garcia, unidentified, Shine Rowan, unidentified, Leslie Howell, Lee Bennett, Paul Harris, and Bud
Smith.

Guests and employees in front of the main lodge at the
Bar F X, the site of Wickenburg's first guest ranch.

Patio at the Remuda Ranch, circa 1929.

Interior of the main lodge at the Monte Vista Ranch, circa 1928.

Auto court on Tegner Street, 1942.

View of Center Street, looking east toward the
river, circa 1940.

Souvenir shop operated by the Round-Up Club
at the intersection of Valentine and Center
streets, sometime in the 1940s.

Wickenburg rodeo, 1940s.

Riders leaving town for the third Desert Caballeros
ride, 1949.

Street scene in 1963.

6 Tourism and the Growth of Modern Wickenburg

WHEN JAPANESE BOMBERS ATTACKED Pearl Harbor in December 1941, plunging the United States into the Second World War, Wickenburg was a quiet roadside town with a thousand residents. Like other small communities in Arizona, it had yet to recover from the depression that had gripped the nation for the last decade; the town's only bank was closed and its traditional industries—ranching and mining—were struggling. In recent years, tourist development had helped keep the town afloat. However, catering to visitors was a relatively new activity for the town, so it was difficult to predict how much Wickenburg could rely on tourist dollars in the future.

Yet only seven years after Pearl Harbor, in 1948, a researcher studying Wickenburg's schools found the town enjoying boom conditions: real estate sales were brisk, new motor courts and curio shops were going up, cars streamed by on the highway through town, and the local population had nearly doubled. "All of these things together have given the community an air of prosperity and well-being it has never felt before in all its history," Jack Fishleder later wrote.

What had happened to produce such a dramatic change in the town's fortunes? In a word, war. Although Wickenburg participated to some extent in the boom fueled by government spending on military supplies and training facilities, the real significance of the wartime economy for the town was the prosperity it brought after hostilities had ceased. Eager to spend their wartime savings, middle-class Americans began traveling in record numbers, and many found their way to Arizona. To meet their demands for facilities and services, new guest ranches, motels, restaurants, souvenir shops, gasoline stations, and other familiar features of the tourist trade were needed in Wickenburg, as were new residents to own and staff the town's businesses.

Wickenburg in Wartime

With one modest exception—a pilot training academy—Wickenburg did not participate directly in the wartime boom that so dramatically transformed other parts of the West. In fact, it first appeared that the war would only hurt the town's economy. As men left to join the armed forces and women were drawn to higher-paying jobs in the new defense industries springing up around Phoenix, local employers—ranches, mines, and other businesses—were forced to contend with periodic labor shortages. Furthermore, the town's dependence on automobile traffic for much of its business left it vulnerable to the effects of government rationing; as the supplies of gasoline and automobile tires available for consumer purchase dwindled, so did the tourist trade. The guest ranches, which had weathered the Depression without much difficulty, now were forced to make the kinds of adjustments that other businesses had made during the 1930s. "Naturally we find that operation of Remuda at present is rather difficult, and sometimes extremely difficult," Sophie Burden advised her clients in the ranch's newsletter for 1943. In addition to struggling to keep its employees, she wrote, Remuda Ranch had been forced to drop its automobile service to and from Phoenix and to cancel all sightseeing trips.

The privations experienced by the guest ranches and other tourist businesses paled in comparison to those suffered by local mines. In 1942, the federal government ordered precious metal mines throughout the West to close so that capital and resources used by them could be diverted to mining and processing industrial metals such as bauxite (for aluminum), iron, tungsten, and manganese. As a result, such local landmarks as the Octave, Congress, and Vulture mines were shut down and, in some cases, their machinery sold for scrap metal. When the closure order arrived at the Vulture, a small crew of men was at work with steam shovels and dump trucks in yet another attempt to extract new riches from the ore dumps and tailings on the property. Expecting to return soon, the men simply walked away from the mine, leaving the machinery and tools that remain at the mine site today. The mine closures, which remained in effect throughout the war, effectively ended Wickenburg's days as a mining center. Once the war was over, an increasing number of residents and business owners began to view new mining development as incompatible with the area's tourist and recreation businesses.

In April 1942, though, the town received some welcome news: Wickenburg had been selected as the site of a new glider pilot training school to be built by the Army Air Force. The Arizona Gliding Academy, as it was called, was not a military base but a civilian-run school operating under a contract with the army to train pilots for a new glider program established to drop men and supplies behind enemy lines. In June 1942, Henry C. Claiborne, a flight instructor during the First World War and now a captain in the Army Air Force reserves, arrived in Wickenburg to begin setting up the school. At first the Fifth Army Air Force Glider Training Detachment was based at Remuda Ranch, which rented most of its rooms to the academy, but soon it moved to temporary quarters on Railroad Street (now Frontier Street) across from the Santa Fe station. Over the summer, a dirt airstrip was constructed west of town on land once owned by the Echeverria family, and a complex of buildings—hangars, barracks, offices, and dispensary—was erected on an adjacent tract known as the Forepaugh property. Later, a second runway was added at the main field and a second landing field was built near Aguila.

By the fall of 1942, school personnel had moved from their temporary offices and quarters in town to those at the airfield, and the school's first classes had arrived for training. Each week brought a new class, with between eighty and ninety students, and the skies were soon filled with gliders and tow planes as the cadets trained day and night. With so many men moving through the school—almost 350 were graduated each month—the Arizona Gliding Academy was a beehive of activity that brought a substantial amount of money into Wickenburg in the form of employee salaries, construction contracts, and spending by off-duty trainees. However, the demand for glider pilots was soon satisfied, and the army decided to close the academy in early 1943 (its last class graduated in January). Fortunately for Wickenburg, the academy was converted to a conventional pilot training school—the Claiborne Flight Academy—and operated as such until the end of the war. In 1946, the facility was declared surplus; a year later, the army turned over the field—constructed at an original cost of $817,000—to the town, thereby giving Wickenburg its first municipal airport.

Wickenburg and the Postwar Boom

Like hundreds of other communities across the West, Wickenburg was brought out of the Depression and to the brink of prosperity by the wartime economy. Fueled by federal government spending on a scale never before seen in American history, the nation's economy was transformed almost overnight; factories, farms, and businesses ran at full capacity, unemployment virtually disappeared, and wages rose. The West was the greatest beneficiary of this increase in government spending, for it was here that many of the new military installations and defense plants were built. In Arizona alone, more than $450 million was spent between 1940 and 1945 on defense-related contracts.

However, following the war's conclusion in 1945, few Americans expected the wartime boom to continue. Most assumed they would pick up their lives where they had left them in 1941 and carry on their affairs much as they had before the war. Indeed, many were worried that demobilization of the nation's armed forces and closure of defense industries would produce a postwar recession much like the one that had struck in the 1920s, after the First World War, and which had been especially severe in Arizona's copper-mining communities.

These concerns proved unwarranted. Rather than demobilizing completely, the United States, fearful of the military strength of the Soviet Union and determined to lead the non-communist nations of the world in a struggle with the Soviets and their allies, continued to maintain substantial armed forces and to spend large amounts of money on weapons and military facilities. More importantly, the nation's economy emerged from the war as the largest, strongest, and richest in the world. Those defense plants not needed for the Cold War military buildup converted to civilian production and soon found a ready market among American workers who had been unable to dispose of their wages during the war because of rationing. Eager to spend their savings, Americans bought refrigerators, stoves, houses, automobiles, and consumer goods in record amounts.

Removed as it was from the economic heartland of the country, Arizona was only partially affected by this industrial boom (though it did benefit from continued military spending). But there was another aspect of postwar prosperity that had a direct and major impact on the state, and especially on Wickenburg: increased mobility. With war veterans who had trained in Arizona and fallen in love with the state's climate and scenery leading the way, new residents began arriving in the state in unprecedented numbers. Most of them settled in the Phoenix and Tucson areas, where the greater proportion of new jobs were created, but some came to Wickenburg and other small towns across Arizona.

More important to Wickenburg were the tourists who came from as near as Phoenix and as far away as the East Coast. Enticed by the new highways built across the country during the Depression and war years, proud of their newly acquired automobiles, and eager to see their country firsthand, middle-class Americans began traveling as never before. Many of them came to the West, attracted by the national parks, distinctive scenery, and—thanks to advertising by western states—a chance to experience the last remnants of the frontier and the "Wild West." In Wickenburg and virtually every other

Arizona community, this expanded tourist trade nurtured such local service businesses as restaurants, motels, gas stations, souvenir shops, and western clothing stores, as well as the contractors, workers, and real estate agents who helped assemble the new tourist infrastructure. Of course, Wickenburg still retained its traditional resource-based industries—ranching, irrigation agriculture (in the Aguila Valley), and a few isolated mining ventures—but these had lost their earlier dominance. Tourism was now the engine that powered Wickenburg's economy.

In 1940, just under a thousand persons were living in Wickenburg; by 1950, that number had jumped to 1,736—the largest increase in the town's population in its ninety-year history. Ten years later, in 1960, there were 2,445 persons living in town, with an estimated 4,000 more residing nearby, in the rural areas and small communities that Wickenburg officials claimed as the town's natural trade area.

As the town's population rose, so did the demand for new services. In 1946, Phoenix-based Valley National Bank opened a branch in Wickenburg, ending a thirteen-year period during which no banking services had been available locally. In 1947, a new town hall was built on Apache Street (where the town-county building is now located); in addition to the town's modest government offices, it also housed a library, which had been established on a permanent footing only five years earlier. New growth naturally meant more school-age children, and the local school systems responded by increasing staff and facilities. In 1951, the high school hired its first full-time principal. Five years later, in 1956, the town's second elementary school was built and named after H. K. MacLennan, a longtime superintendent of the elementary district. Meanwhile, the town had been slowly outgrowing the small post office on Railroad Street; it was replaced in 1961 by a new post office on Yavapai Street (which itself was replaced in 1996 by a facility on west Wickenburg Way).

The growth was reflected in other institutions as well. In 1952, the First Presbyterian Church completed work on a new sanctuary and building to replace the one built in 1921, and in 1957 the local Catholic church, St. Anthony of Padua, replaced its existing adobe building, which dated from 1902. That same year, the Wickenburg Community Hospital was completed, replacing a small, privately-run facility that at one point had been located at Center (now Wickenburg Way) and Jefferson streets. Of perhaps greater importance, at least for the local economy, were the new automobile courts and motels. As the number of middle-class tourists increased rapidly, so did the need for affordable lodging; by 1955, there were twenty motels in and near the town. Unlike the guest ranches, which were on the outskirts of Wickenburg, these establishments were located in town, which helped stimulate the growth of other businesses such as restaurants, cafes, and souvenir shops.

Guest Ranching After the War

The revival of the travel industry after the war benefited the guest ranches as well; indeed, for the guest ranch industry as a whole in Arizona, the late 1940s were boom years. By 1948, there were 153 guest ranches scattered across the state, with more than half of them concentrated near Phoenix, Tucson, and Wickenburg. Although Wickenburg still claimed to be the "Dude Ranch Capital of the World," by this time there were actually more ranches in the Tucson area. By itself, the question of which community had the most guest ranches was little more than a matter of bragging rights. But the increasing importance of Tucson as a guest ranch hub reflected several changes taking place in the industry that later had important consequences for Wickenburg's oldest tourist attractions. As guest ranch patrons demanded more comfortable, resort-like accommodations, small towns like Wickenburg found it harder to compete with urban areas that could offer a choice of golf courses, better shopping, and a wider variety of restaurants and nightclubs.

At war's end, though, it seemed that nothing but growth lay ahead for Wickenburg's guest ranches. In 1947, the Slash Bar K was opened by a Chicago couple, Donald and Margaret Kerr, and the Flying E began operations under owner Lee Eyerly. Later acquired by George and Vi Wellik in 1952, the Flying E eventually became one of the largest guest ranches in the area, with more than 17,000 acres of land. In 1948, the Rancho de los Caballeros was established by several winter visitors—Sylvia and C. L. "Squire" Maguire, and Rowena and Belford Howard—in partnership with a former Remuda Ranch employee, Dallas Gant Sr., who with his wife Edith managed the new ranch. Set up on a tract of land west of town and south of US Highway 60, Rancho de los Caballeros pointed the way toward many of the changes that later took place in the Wickenburg guest ranch industry. In addition to offering fully heated rooms with private baths—by now standard for guest ranches—the new enterprise incorporated several features long associated with resorts: a swimming pool, tennis court, putting green, and poolside dining area.

As the ranches embraced new recreational pursuits such as swimming and golf, their emphasis on some of the traditional guest ranch activities waned. One casualty was the ranch-sponsored rodeos, which were gradually dropped in favor of much smaller festivities, known as "gymkhana," that consisted primarily of games played on horseback. By the end of the war, ranch owners were beginning to doubt the wisdom of staging rodeos, largely because of their expense. They also were looking for ways to keep winter visitors in town at the end of the season. And so, after deciding in January 1947 to end their sponsorship of a three-day springtime rodeo that the Remuda and other ranches had hosted for some time, a group of guest ranchers and town business owners organized a multi-day springtime horseback ride. Calling themselves the Desert Caballeros, the group held its first ride in the spring of 1947.

Blazing a trail into the western foothills of the Bradshaw Mountains and scouting out campsites, the Desert Caballeros organizers set up a route that the riders covered in several days, thus establishing a pattern for the rides that has been followed up to the present. Each day, the riders, who paid a handsome fee to participate in the event, made their way up the trail on horseback while their gear was loaded on trucks and driven ahead to the next campsite. There, a group of hired hands—usually guest ranch employees and local cowboys—set up camp and awaited the riders. No women were allowed on the rides, which over time assumed the character of a multi-day party in the desert. To keep the inconveniences of camp life from dampening the festive atmosphere, the accommodations were anything but Spartan; full bars, entertainment stages, sound and lighting systems, electrical generators, beds, air mattresses, and other amenities soon became standard gear for the Desert Caballeros rides. Over the years, the ride has received a considerable amount of local and even national press coverage, much of it slyly poking fun at the elaborate preparations made by ride organizers on behalf of the wealthy executives and professional men who have composed the lion's share of the rider corps.

Not to be outdone, a group of women—winter visitors, local residents, and business owners—set up a similar organization, Las Damas, which began sponsoring trail rides for women in 1948. Unlike the men's group, Las Damas did not move its camp from place to place each evening; instead, the organizers established a base camp somewhere in the desert hills near town and then went out on a series of daylong trail rides, eventually returning to the camp each night. In most other respects, though, the ride was similar to that of the Desert Caballeros: hired hands brought gear and supplies in by truck and set up camp for the riders, and a substantial fee was required of participants.

Ironically, as the Desert Caballeros and Las Damas were beginning long and successful runs as two of Wickenburg's main seasonal events, the guest ranches that had helped organize them were entering a period of moderate instability. The tourist industry was by its very nature volatile, and ranches frequently changed hands or closed down. Even the most venerable ranches were not exempt. In 1946, Lewis C. "Bob" White, who helped establish the first Remuda Ranch, sold his Monte Vista Ranch to a Denver couple who continued its operation as a guest ranch. That same year, the Triangle W, a ten-year-old guest ranch, also changed hands. As part of that deal, the original owners, Charles and Helen Williams, kept half of the ranch acreage and developed it as the C4 subdivision, while the new owners continued to operate the guest ranch.

During this period, the establishment of the Slash Bar K, Flying E, and Rancho de los Caballeros did not significantly increase the number of guest ranches in the Wickenburg area, though the construction of Rancho de los Caballeros did bring a major increase in the number of guest ranch rooms. As a result, the number of ranches, if not their ownership, remained static; by 1955, there were eight guest ranches in the area—only one more than in 1938. Nine years later, in 1964, there were still eight ranches: the Diamond P, Flying E, Kay El Bar, Lazy Fox (formerly the Triangle W), Monte Vista, Rancho de los Caballeros, Slash Bar K, and Remuda. A year later, though, the Monte Vista—a local tourist landmark since 1926—was closed; eventually the ranch buildings were converted into apartments. By 1969, the Triangle W and Lazy Fox had gone out of business, and later that year, the Remuda Ranch—the area's oldest guest ranch—was sold by longtime owner Sophie Burden. With the addition of one new ranch, Rancho Casitas, that left seven ranches in the Wickenburg area as the 1970s began—the same as before the war.

What these shifts in ownership reflected, more than anything else, was the competitive pressure being applied to guest ranches not only in Wickenburg, but everywhere across the West. "The other ranches [that survived] were changing hands rapidly at this time and getting new managers and starting to build up," observed Pete Fletcher, the longtime manager of the Remuda Ranch. "People were more interested in the recreation facilities and the guest ranches' occupation as entertainment centers became less interesting and the business died down. Many of the guest ranches went out of business or changed into the resort type." Guests were more demanding now, and they wanted to do more than ride horses and go on cookouts with the ranch wranglers. In part, this reflected shifts in taste; re-creations of the "Old West" no longer had quite the appeal they once did. But it also reflected changing vacation and recreation habits. Whereas guest ranch patrons once came for the entire season, often bringing their families, now they were too occupied with work and other commitments to take more than a two- or three-week vacation. In addition, they had acquired new recreational interests—hiking, tennis, and golf—that were better accommodated by resorts. Some guest ranchers responded to this pressure by retiring or selling out, others by changing their facilities and even their marketing gambits. The Slash Bar K, for example, began promoting itself as a "health ranch" and "complete health spa" to such an extent that it barely qualified as a guest ranch in the traditional sense of the term. By offering such services as physical therapy and residential nursing care, the Slash Bar K had come to embrace the very customers—convalescents—that the first guest ranches, founded when tuberculosis was common, took great pains to keep away.

Diversifying the Local Economy

The steady growth of Wickenburg in the late 1940s and 1950s, which brought new residents and businesses to town, left the town larger and more prosperous than it had ever been in its hundred-year history. But the town once again depended on one industry, tourism, which was hardly known for its stability. With tourist development accelerating in the rest of Arizona and throughout the Southwest, Wickenburg's attractions were no longer as unique as they once were. The proliferation of tourist attractions in the West combined with other trends—the rise of national motel chains and the construction of the interstate highway system—to bring increasing competitive pressure on Wickenburg and its lodging industry. In 1955, there were twenty motels and tourist courts in town. By 1964, the number had dropped to seventeen, and five years later, in 1969, there were only fourteen motels in town.

With through traffic no longer showing the annual increases it once had, business growth slowed, as did the rate of immigration; during the 1960s, the town's population increased by only thirty persons a year. More importantly, the area's population—on which the business community of Wickenburg depended—appeared to have stabilized at around seven thousand. This had important implications for the town's non-tourist businesses, which also faced competition from shopping centers and stores in the steadily expanding Phoenix metropolitan area. As if to dramatize this change, the Brayton Commercial Company store on Railroad Street, for years the shopping hub of Wickenburg, closed its doors on 30 July 1966. Brayton's had long before stopped selling groceries, at about the same time that a new Safeway store opened in town in 1955; now the venerable hardware and dry goods store was unable to compete altogether. Three years after closing, in 1969, Brayton's was converted into a history museum, the Desert Caballeros Western Museum.

Recognizing that diversification of the local economy was necessary to keep Wickenburg from suffering another downturn of the sort that had crippled the town in the 1880s and 1920s—when it was dependent on another unstable industry, mining—the town's business and government leaders began advertising Wickenburg's climate and "quality of life" in hopes of attracting light industry and year-round residents. In 1964, the town government opened an industrial air park adjacent to the airport on the western edge of town. Wickenburg was especially successful in attracting new residents, most of them retirees lured by the Sunbelt's climate, relaxed lifestyle, and affordable housing. The Remuda Ranch and Rancho de los Caballeros already had demonstrated the appeal of Wickenburg to wealthy retirees and second-home owners by carving subdivisions out of their acreage for sale to current and former guests. In 1964, for example, the Remuda Ranchettes opened for sale, offering "fully restricted" homesites with good roads and full town services.

By the early 1970s, retirees and part-time residents were a significant part of Wickenburg's population and economic base. Each winter, their arrival caused the town's population to mushroom from 2,600 to more than 6,000. Although this trend could be seen in many other cities and towns across the Southwest, Wickenburg stood out among Arizona communities because a noticeably large proportion of its new residents were wealthy. The guest ranches for years had attracted the prominent and well-to-do to Wickenburg; now these visitors began to build first or second homes in and around the town, taking up residence either full-time or during the winter.

With new home construction booming and the wintertime tourist trade holding steady, Wickenburg's population once again rose during the 1970s, when it increased 31 percent, to 3,535 in 1980. To meet the demands imposed by this growth, the town built a new community center (1971) and library (1972), both of which remain in use today. Wickenburg also acquired a new museum building, though not under happy circumstances. In December 1972, a fire destroyed the old Brayton Commercial building, leaving the Desert Caballeros Western Museum with neither a home nor a collection. At first the town was in shock; many residents had donated memorabilia, antiques, artwork, photographs, and other personal items that were lost in the fire. But soon the town mobilized to build a new museum, a task that was completed in three years with volunteer labor and the donation of yet more artifacts and memorabilia.

Challenges to Wickenburg's Tourist Trade

Although the town failed to attract light industry and other new businesses as quickly as it would have liked—the industrial air park did not get its first tenant until 1971—the spurt in second-home construction and the relocation of retirees to Wickenburg helped diversify the town's economy enough that it was no longer entirely dependent on the tourist trade. This was fortunate, for in the early 1960s, Wickenburg was confronted with the prospect that its basic industry, tourism, might be undercut by plans to build a new highway in Arizona as part of the evolving federal interstate highway system. For an old mining town such as Wickenburg, this was a familiar story: men in distant capitals were making decisions that would determine the fate of the town, with the only difference being that the decision-makers were now highway engineers in Phoenix rather than mining investors in New York.

At issue was the future route of the cross-country interstate highway that would eventually replace US 60, which passed through Wickenburg on its way to the West Coast from Phoenix. By 1960, the Arizona Highway Commission was studying two alternate routes for the highway, which was to be called Interstate 10: the existing route followed by US 60, and another that extended directly west from Phoenix, passing well to the south of Wickenburg and rejoining US 60 near the town of Brenda. The Brenda Cutoff, as it was soon dubbed, was vigorously opposed by Wickenburg officials and business owners, but to no avail; in November 1961, the Highway Commission announced its decision to build the cutoff, citing as explanation the need to meet the "higher" design standards—fewer curves and hills— established for the interstate system. As compensation for eventually depriving Wickenburg of its main source of tourists, the commission agreed to delay construction of the new road until after the rest of the state's interstate highways had been completed. It also promised to build a new highway, Arizona 74, that would restore some of Wickenburg's lost tourist traffic by connecting the town directly to Interstate 17, the new highway being built between Phoenix and Flagstaff.

Not surprisingly, Wickenburg residents remained apprehensive about the change. "The Brenda Cutoff will cut us out of our regular source of cash," a town official complained in 1967. "Through traffic is our economic base." When the new I-10 was finally opened in 1973, all of the worse predictions seemed to be borne out as traffic on US 60 dropped by half. Two years later, Wickenburg town officials reported a 10 percent drop in sales tax revenues and a 50 percent decrease in traffic. Three motels had closed, one restaurant had converted to a clothing store, and the remaining service businesses—gas stations, restaurants, motels, and the like—were all feeling the pressure of reduced patronage. "The town began clawing and is still groping for an antidote," an *Arizona Republic* reporter observed.

What saved Wickenburg was its growing reputation as a wintertime destination for wealthy retirees and vacationers. Construction of new homes proceeded at a brisk pace. "Many multimillionaires, millionaires, and near-millionaires live in and around Wickenburg," an *Arizona Gazette* reporter wrote in 1977 after visiting the town. "Just drive off the main roads and you'll see their fancy homes." As the reporter concluded in his article, which was headlined "Wickenburg Is Alive and Well," the town's future lay not with the transient tourist trade but with residential development and the cultivation of

Wickenburg as a tourist destination—a distinction that would place the guest ranches once again at the center of the area's tourist economy. In 1974, the Wickenburg Inn Tennis and Guest Ranch opened on a large expanse of desert well outside the town's limits. Although it was not a guest ranch in the usual sense of the term—it placed more emphasis on tennis than on riding—it did attract the same stratum of tourists as did the guest ranches, and it was the largest guest facility ever built in the area.

Otherwise, the guest ranch industry was going through yet another period of change, this one rather unsettling in its consequences. As the opening of the Wickenburg Inn signaled, the pendulum in the tourist industry was swinging farther away from riding and other "western" activities (in which guest ranches excelled) to less regionally specific activities such as golf, hiking, swimming, sightseeing, and shopping (which were the province of resorts). Recognizing this trend, the Rancho de los Caballeros made several improvements in 1979 that included construction of a nine-hole golf course (later expanded to eighteen holes), clubhouse, pro shop, and driving range. Some of the other guest ranches managed to hold their own, but it was increasingly clear that the guest ranch industry was not what it had once been. By the early 1970s, the Remuda Ranch was being run under the European plan, its dining room converted to a restaurant. And the old Garden of Allah site—which had been operated as the Circle Flying W and Lazy R C guest ranches, among others—was now a trailer park and campground called the Shady River-Palm Lake Guest Ranch. In 1975, there were seven guest ranches operating in the area—the same number as in 1938.

The Demise of a "Western" Town?

To some, these changes in the guest ranch industry signaled a larger shift in the community away from its roots as a "western" town. Even in the mid-1960s, Sophie Burden, the longtime proprietor of the Remuda Ranch, had voiced her concern that the town was losing its distinctive character. "Our town lost far too much of its flavor when it got so you could drive through town and not see one person in western dress," she wrote to a fellow business owner. "People come here so they can be comfortable and dress as they like—and they like western dress—and they complain to me (because they know I agree) that nobody else dresses western, so they are embarrassed to." Ten years later, a reporter for the *Arizona Republic* made much the same observation. "There are as many warm up suits and tennies as there are boots, big hats and jeans," he wrote. "You can count almost as many antiques-and-arts emporiums as saloons, and for every three mobile homes in town, there's at least one $100,000 pad in the rolling desert hills of the suburbs." That same year, 1975, Dana Burden, the head of Wickenburg's Chamber of Commerce (which no longer was called the Round-Up Club), formally conceded the title of "Dude Ranch Capital of the World" to Tucson—a concession of symbolic, if not practical, import.

Although it might have seemed to longtime Wickenburg residents that this shift away from their western roots was peculiar to their town, in fact similar changes were taking place all across the West. For that matter, communities in many of the country's regions—New England, the South, the Midwest—seemed gradually to be losing their distinctiveness in food, attire, manners, customs, and speech patterns. In the case of Wickenburg and other small towns in the West, this sense of eroding regional identity developed as the West was gradually drawn into the economic and social mainstream of the nation following the Second World War.

It also did not help that the tourists who came through Wickenburg now measured their stays in days rather than weeks, even at the guest ranches; investing time and money in "going native" seemed rather extravagant for shorter stays, with the result that fewer tourists dressed and acted "western" while in town. Perhaps most importantly, Americans were not as keenly interested in the "Old West" as they had once been; Western television shows and movies had lost much of their earlier popularity, and travelers to the West now were drawn to fitness-related activities like tennis, hiking, golf, and camping as much as they were to riding and ranch life.

As a result of these and related changes, Wickenburg's appeal to tourists and prospective residents shifted; now, in the 1970s, its main attraction was something that publications like *Sunset* magazine called the "western lifestyle," which emphasized climate, outdoor living, and recreational pursuits that extended far beyond riding. The town also increasingly emphasized its small-town character in a way that had nothing to do with its location. Pointing to the absence of industry and other urban features, advertisers for the town and its businesses sought to entice some of the retirees and others who were beginning to migrate to the less populated states of the West from urban areas in the Northeast and Midwest (and from California as well). The essence of this appeal was revealed clearly in a mid-1970s advertisement for Westpark, a new mobile home development in Wickenburg, which invited retirees to the "No-No World of Wickenburg": "no smog borne ills, nor traffic chills, no chlorine to drink, nor industrial stink, no racial blaspheme, nor weather extreme, no bug-a-boo scars on the beauty in view."

The reference to "scars" was especially telling, given Wickenburg's past as a mining town. The town's business owners and residents once eagerly greeted any hint of a revival in the area's flagging mining fortunes, but now they were beginning to doubt the wisdom—on both economic and aesthetic grounds—of allowing any mining activity that might mar the scenery responsible for so much of the town's recent growth. The depth of this change in sentiment was made clear in 1977, when reports surfaced that more than a dozen major oil and mining concerns were buying uranium claims in the Date Creek Mountains north of town. One company, the Union Oil Corporation, announced plans to bring in as many as two hundred workers, a move that might increase the population of Wickenburg by a thousand persons. According to Dana Burden, head of the Chamber of Commerce, the town had mixed feelings about the project. "People have a lot of reservations," he told a Phoenix reporter. "What is a thousand people going to do to us?" The uranium boom fizzled out before any of the development came, but it still left town residents divided over the wisdom of welcoming any economic activity that might make the area less attractive to retirees and tourists. According to one local observer, the publisher of the *Wickenburg Sun*, the dispute spawned pro- and anti-growth factions, with retirees taking a prominent role in the latter group.

As Wickenburg moved into the new decade, it soon became clear that the town was in the midst of another period of sustained growth, perhaps the longest in its history. After growing more than 30 percent between 1970 and 1980, the town's population continued to increase. By 1985, there were nearly four thousand permanent residents, of whom more than a third (34 percent) were retirees. By 1990, the number had risen to forty-five hundred, with another four thousand persons living within a half-hour's drive of Wickenburg.

Reflecting these increases, the town's economy grew as well, though not in quite the balanced fashion that town officials and business owners might have wanted. As it had been for much of its past, Wickenburg remained primarily a service community; now, instead of groceries and supplies for miners and ranchers, the town's bread-and-butter was a wide array of goods and services for retirees, winter visitors, and tourists, supplemented by sales to a trade area of permanent residents estimated to contain as many as eighteen thousand persons. Located on the major highway between Phoenix and Las Vegas, US 93, Wickenburg continued to see a steady stream of travelers. Although the number of guest ranches had shrunk to five by 1987 (the Flying E, Rancho Casitas, Kay El Bar, Rancho de los Caballeros, and Wickenburg Inn Tennis and Guest Ranch), expansion at the latter two helped keep the number of rooms from dropping precipitously. In all, tourism supported more than a hundred businesses in Wickenburg.

However, as Wickenburg residents were learning, the business of catering to retirees and tourists had gradually but significantly changed the structure of the town's economy. In 1984, construction, retail, and service businesses accounted for 85 percent of the town's jobs. Mining and agriculture, once the mainstays of Wickenburg's economy, now provided less than 5 percent of its jobs, while industry accounted for only 2.5 percent. Wickenburg was not alone in experiencing this shift to a service economy, which was national in scope but especially apparent in the West. Still, that was not much consolation for Wickenburg's new generation of workers. Dismayed by the low wages that typified employment in the service sector, many found the town an inhospitable environment in which to begin their careers. "Upon graduation from high school the community's young people leave the area in pursuit of opportunity," a town report noted, with most gravitating toward the Phoenix metropolitan area.

Wickenburg also found itself struggling with another consequence of growth, namely, the decline of the central part of the town. Like other communities in Arizona, Wickenburg had gradually seen its businesses migrate outward from the old downtown to the highways leading in and out of town. This process was accelerated in Wickenburg by the construction of new residential developments, to the west and south, that attracted not only residents but businesses as well. By 1984, Wickenburg's downtown was no longer the area's shopping hub; most of the businesses that had once lined Frontier and Tegner streets were gone, leaving many of the storefronts vacant. "Historic downtown Wickenburg is on a one-way, downhill slide into overwhelming blight," a town report concluded, pointing in particular to the area between Center, Tegner, Yavapai, and Frontier streets.

As has happened in many other cities and towns across the country, Wickenburg's officials and residents found that the most direct route to the revitalization of the downtown led backward, into the past. Tourists and new residents alike had long been drawn to local historic features such as the Vulture Mine and other reminders of the region's mining past. If improvements were made to the downtown, town officials and business owners reasoned, Wickenburg's historic buildings and friendly small-town atmosphere might prove to be similarly attractive to tourists, whose presence would eventually coax businesses back into the area.

In 1982, the town council established a Downtown Revitalization and Historic Preservation Task Force. As its first project, the task force coordinated the repaving and landscaping of Frontier Street, which was completed in early 1983. Over the next two years, the old shopping district between Frontier and Tegner streets was gradually transformed; using federal grant money and town funds, the town paved alleys, buried utility wires, and added parking spaces. Also, the old Santa Fe (formerly the Santa Fe, Prescott & Phoenix) railroad depot was restored and taken over by the Chamber of Commerce for use as a visitor's center and office. In 1985, a consulting firm hired by the town completed a survey of historic buildings that identified more than twenty-five properties that were architecturally or historically distinctive. One of them, the Garcia School (formerly the Wickenburg Grammar School), was already on the National Register of Historic Places, but the others were still unprotected. By 1986, an additional twenty-six buildings—including the railroad depot, Vernetta Hotel, first town hall and jail, Echeverria house, and high school—had been placed on the National Register.

Over time, a few of Wickenburg's historic buildings have been lost to decay or demolition; the Baxter Opera House, for example, was demolished by the Desert Caballeros Western Museum to make way for the park and statue that now stands at the intersection of Wickenburg Way and Tegner. Still, by the mid-1990s, the number of protected historic buildings had grown to thirty-two. And, perhaps more importantly, the downtown was enjoying new life as tourists and residents alike rediscovered the simple pleasures of strolling and shopping on streets laid out when the railroad was still the principal means of intercity transportation.

The downtown has not been the only historic feature of Wickenburg to receive renewed attention in recent years. Tourists new to the area might find it hard to believe that the Hassayampa River was once the lifeblood of Wickenburg when it was a small farming and mining community. But there is one section south of town where the river flows year-round, its waters forced upward by bedrock that rises to the surface. An oasis in the desert—it was once Frederick Brill's home-stead and, later, the Garden of Allah guest ranch—this thickly veg-etated stretch of river was in danger of being sold to a gravel mining company in the mid-1980s. Concerned that a vital part of Arizona's human and natural heritage might be lost, the Arizona Nature Conservancy bought the property in 1987 and established the Hassayampa River Preserve.

Now, residents and visitors who wish to experience the Hassayampa River valley as it was before the gold miners arrived in the 1860s can visit the preserve's spring-fed pond and groves, which offer a shady respite from the desert's summer heat. Here they will glimpse remnants of the cottonwood and mesquite forests that once lined the river for miles in either direction and provided early miners with the fuel they needed for their stamp mills, the wildlife and seasonal plants that led the Yavapai Indians to establish so many *rancherias* along the river, and the flowing water that has provided drinking and irrigation water to generations of inhabitants. The Hassayampa River has changed considerably over the years—nothing will bring back the rich farming soil washed away in the Walnut Grove Dam flood—yet it still flows past Wickenburg, a living link to the town's rich and colorful past as a farming, mining, and tourist community.

Chronology of
Wickenburg History

1598   Marcos Farfán de los Godos is first European to meet Yavapai Indians

1776   Franciscan monk Francisco Garcés visits Yavapai Indians while journeying across desert to California

1863   Prospecting party led by Abraham Peeples and Pauline Weaver discovers gold at Rich Hill

       Henry Wickenburg and two other men discover Vulture Mine

1863–64   Warfare with Yavapai Indians begins near settlement of Weaver

1864   Wickenburg Mining District formed

       Vulture Mine begins production

       Settlement established at Wickenburg Ranch, later called Wickenburg

1865   First stamp mill in Wickenburg erected on Martinez Wash

       Henry Wickenburg sells Vulture Mine to New York investors who form Vulture Mining Company

       Post office established at Wickenburg

       Yavapai Indians agree to settle on Colorado River reservation

1867   Camp Date Creek established by U.S. Army

1868	Wickenburg townsite laid out and first town lots sold
1871	Yavapai Indian reservation established at Camp Date Creek
	Stage holdup known as Wickenburg Massacre results in death of seven persons
1872	Gen. George Crook begins army offensive against Yavapai Indians
	Settlement established at Seymour after stamp mill moved there from Wickenburg
1873	Warfare with Yavapai Indians ends and Yavapai sent to Rio Verde reservation
	Vulture Mine closes for first time
1875	Yavapai Indians sent to the San Carlos Apache reservation
1878	Central Arizona Mining Company reopens Vulture Mine
1879	Wickenburg's first school established
1880	Mill at Seymour shut down
1884	Vulture Mine closes for second time
1890	Walnut Grove Dam breaks and floods Hassayampa River valley, killing between fifty and seventy persons
	Garcia Cemetery established
1891	Congress Mine begins full production
	Santa Fe, Prescott & Phoenix Railroad (SFP&P) established
1895	Wickenburg railroad depot built and service inaugurated along SFP&P line between Ash Fork and Phoenix
1896	Castle Hot Springs resort opens
1897	Wickenburg townsite formally surveyed and official plat recorded
	Vulture Mine sold in tax sale to Vulture Mining Company
1901	*Wickenburg News-Herald*, town's first newspaper, established
1902	First telephone service in town

Adobe sanctuary built by members of St. Anthony of Padua Catholic Church

1905   Vernetta Hotel built

Wickenburg Grammar School (later the Garcia School) erected

First Presbyterian Church established

Henry Wickenburg commits suicide

1906   Brayton Commercial Company established

1909   Town of Wickenburg incorporated

1911   Congress Mine shuts down

1912   Garden of Allah resort opens

1914   Wickenburg's first bank, Traders' Bank, opens

First bridge across Hassayampa River constructed

1917   Municipal water system begins service

1918   Municipal electric plant begins operation

1922   US Highways 60 and 89 established

1923–24   First guest ranch, Bar F X ranch, opens for one season

1925   Remuda Ranch, first full-time guest ranch, opens

1926   Monte Vista Ranch opens

1927   Kay El Bar begins operation as full-time guest ranch

1928   Wickenburg High School opens

1934   Paving of US Highway 60 completed

1935   Paving of US Highway 89 completed

1937   New bridge across Hassayampa River constructed

1942   Arizona Glider Academy established to train army pilots

1946   Valley National Bank, first in Wickenburg since 1930s, opens town branch

1947   Glider academy field given to Wickenburg for municipal airport

New town hall built on Apache Street

Slash Bar K and Flying E guest ranches open

Desert Caballeros organize their first ride

1948	Rancho de los Caballeros guest ranch opens
	Las Damas conduct their first ride
1952	New building erected by First Presbyterian Church
1956	MacLennan Elementary School opens
1957	New building erected by St. Anthony of Padua Catholic Church
	Wickenburg Community Hospital opens
1961	New post office on Yavapai Street opens
	Interstate 10 proposed as new route for southern Arizona's cross-country highway
1966	Brayton Commercial Company closes
1969	Desert Caballeros Western Museum established in Brayton's building
1971	Wickenburg Community Center opens
1972	New town library opens
	Desert Caballeros Western Museum building burns down
1973	Brenda Cutoff on I-10 opens, causing sharp drop in highway traffic through Wickenburg
1974	Wickenburg Inn Tennis and Guest Ranch opens
1975	Desert Caballeros Western Museum reopens in new building
1982	Downtown Revitalization and Historic Preservation Task Force established
1987	Hassayampa River Preserve established by Nature Conservancy

Suggestions for Further Reading

WHAT FOLLOWS IS A SELECTIVE LISTING of items that readers are most likely to find useful should they wish to learn more about Wickenburg's past, rather than a compilation of every source consulted in the preparation of this study. In making this selection, emphasis has been placed on readability and breadth of coverage; ephemera such as newspaper articles, pamphlets, and the like have been excluded except in a few instances.

For general information on the history of Arizona, the best sources are Thomas E. Sheridan's *Arizona: A History* (Tucson: University of Arizona Press, 1995); two books by Jay J. Wagoner, *Early Arizona: Prehistory to Civil War* (University of Arizona Press, 1975) and *Arizona Territory, 1863–1912: A Political History* (University of Arizona Press, 1970); and the *Historical Atlas of Arizona* by Henry P. Walker and Don Bufkin (2d edition; Norman: University of Oklahoma Press, 1986).

A very interesting firsthand account of the Joseph Walker gold-mining party that first explored the Hassayampa River area is found in Daniel Ellis Conner's memoir, *Joseph Reddeford Walker and the Arizona Adventure,* edited by Donald J. Berthrong and Odessa Davenport (Norman: University of Oklahoma Press, 1956).

A concise introduction to the Yavapai Indians can be found in *Paths of Life: American Indians of the Southwest and Northern Mexico,* edited by Thomas E. Sheridan and Nancy J. Parezo (Tucson: University of Arizona Press, 1996). Other sources on the Yavapai include: Sigrid Khera and Patricia S. Mariella, "Yavapai," in volume 10 of the *Handbook of North American Indians*, edited by Alfonso Ortiz (Washington, D.C.: Smithsonian Institution, 1983); E. W. N. Gifford's *Northeastern and Western Yavapai*, University of California Publications in American Archeology and Ethnology 34, no. 4. (Berkeley: University of California Press, 1936); and Albert H. Schroeder, *A Study of Yavapai History* (New York: Garland, 1974).

For information on the military campaign against the Yavapai, see Sidney B. Brinckerhoff, "Camp Date Creek, Arizona Territory: Infantry Outpost in the Yavapai Wars, 1867–1873," *The Smoke Signal* (Fall 1964), published by the Tucson Westerners Corral; and Dan L. Thrapp, *The Conquest of Apacheria* (Norman: University of Oklahoma Press, 1967). An interesting firsthand account of Indian warfare in territorial Arizona that devotes a limited amount of space to the Yavapai is John G. Bourke's memoir, *On the Border with Crook* (1891; Lincoln: University of Nebraska Press, 1971).

There are several sources that describe the early days of Wickenburg, though readers should be advised to use these with caution, as they contain conflicting and sometimes erroneous information. These include Helen B. Hawkins' *A History of Wickenburg to 1875* (Wickenburg, Ariz.: Maricopa County Historical Society, 1971); James M. Barney's "The Early Annals of the Wickenburg Country," a typescript manuscript produced in 1942 (available at the museum's library and also in the James M. Barney Collection at the Arizona Historical Foundation, Hayden Library, Arizona State University, Tempe); and Dan B. Genung, "Reminiscences of Dan B. Genung as Told to Mrs. George F. Kitt, Jan. 19, 1939," manuscript collection no. 284 at the Arizona Historical Society in Tucson. For information on Henry Wickenburg, see the Hayden biographical file under Wickenburg's name at the Luhrs Reading Room, Hayden Library, Arizona State University.

There are any number of sources available on gold mining in central Arizona. By far the best single account of the rise and fall of the Vulture Mine is found in Duane A. Smith's "The Vulture Mine: Arizona's Golden Mirage," *Arizona and the West* 14 (Autumn 1972).

Other books and articles on gold mining are: Robert L. Spude, "The Walker-Weaver Diggings and the Mexican Placero, 1863–1864," *Journal of the West* 14 (October 1975); H. Mason Coggin, "A History of Placer Mining in Arizona," in *History of Mining in Arizona,* edited by J. Michael Canty and Michael N. Greeley (Tucson: Mining Club of the Southwest Foundation, 1987); and Maureen G. Johnson, *Placer Gold Deposits of Arizona,* U. S. Geological Survey Bulletin no. 1355 (Washington, D. C.: Government Printing Office, 1972). An interesting firsthand account of mining in the early years of this century is Frank A. Crampton's *Deep Enough: A Working Stiff in the Western Mine Camps* (1956; Norman: University of Oklahoma Press, 1982). A snapshot of Wickenburg's mining economy in 1905 is provided in *Description of Mines and Prospects near Wickenburg,* compiled by L. C. Nickerson and published by the Wickenburg Business Men and Miners' Association (available at the Arizona Historical Foundation); for a later picture, see O. H. Metzger, *Gold Mining and Milling in the Wickenburg Area, Maricopa and Yavapai Counties, Ariz.* (Bureau of Mines, Department of the Interior, Information Circular 6991, February 1938). Readers can also consult the James M. Barney Collection at the Arizona Historical Foundation, which contains a series of magazine articles Barney wrote on early gold mining in the territorial period, "Arizona's Trail of Gold."

One place to look for information on Wickenburg and the other towns of Arizona is in the many guide books describing the territory and state that have been published over the years. Noteworthy ones include Patrick Hamilton, *The Resources of Arizona,* 3d edition (San Francisco: A. L. Bancroft & Co., 1884); Richard J. Hinton, *The Hand-Book to Arizona: Its Resources, History, Towns, Mines, Ruins, and Scenery* (1878; Tucson: Arizona Silhouettes, 1954); and George Wharton James, *Arizona, the Wonderland* (Boston: Page Co., 1917). Wickenburg's attractions as a winter resort were described by J. B. Priestley in "Arizona Desert: Reflections of a Winter Visitor," *Harper's Magazine* (March 1937).

For a very detailed history of the railroad that served Wickenburg, see John W. Sayre, *The Santa Fe, Prescott, & Phoenix Railway: The*

Scenic Line of Arizona (Boulder, Colo.: Pruett, 1990). The career of the SFP&P's principal backer, Frank Murphy, is described by H. Mason Coggin in "Frank M. Murphy—Arizona Gold Miner," in volume 2 of *History of Mining in Arizona,* edited by J. Michael Canty and Michael N. Greeley (Tucson: Mining Club of the Southwest Foundation, 1991). Anyone interested in tracing the development of central Arizona's highways should consult early issues (from the 1920s and 1930s) of *Arizona Highways* magazine, which initially was devoted not to tourism but to highway construction.

Sadly, there is very little that has been published on the history of tourism in Arizona. As a result, the best sources of information on Wickenburg's guest ranches are promotional brochures, which can be found in several library and archive collections. There are files of pamphlets and brochures on Wickenburg-area guest ranches and on Castle Hot Springs at the Luhrs Reading Room and Arizona Historical Foundation, both at Hayden Library, Arizona State University. Also, the Desert Caballeros Western Museum has an extensive collection of materials on area guest ranches, especially the Remuda Ranch; unfortunately it is not catalogued. A description of the Garden of Allah ("The Garden of Allah: A Comfortable Resort") can be found in *Arizona: The State Magazine* 3 (June 1915).

Various aspects of the town's history are covered in the following items: David B. Dill Jr., "Terror on the Hassayampa: The Walnut Grove Dam Disaster of 1890," *Journal of Arizona History* 28 (Autumn 1987); Jack Fishleder, "The Development of the Wickenburg Public Schools: 1879–1948" (M.A. thesis, University of Arizona, 1948); "Hispanic Pioneers of Wickenburg," supplement to the *Wickenburg Sun,* 7 September 1994; J. Norman Grim, "World War II Glider Pilot Training in Arizona," *Military History of the West* 23, no. 2 (1993); and Nell Simcox, "Brayton's: Arizona's Early 'Chain Stores,'" *True West* (May–June 1980).

Some topics can be researched individually at the Wickenburg Public Library, which has an extensive newspaper clipping and ephemera collection on the town's history. An interesting source of information on Wickenburg in 1915 and 1931 are the insurance maps produced by the Sanborn Map Company. These maps, which show every building and street in the downtown (as well as part of the residential area), are available on microfilm at the Arizona State Library (located at the capitol building in Phoenix) and at Noble Library at Arizona State University.

As always with small towns in Arizona, much of the historical record pertaining to Wickenburg is found in contemporary newspapers. Unfortunately, Wickenburg did not have its own newspaper until 1901; before then, occasional articles on the town could be found only in other Arizona newspapers, especially those published in Phoenix and Prescott. Scattered issues from the various Wickenburg newspapers published between 1901 and 1917—the *Wickenburg News-Herald,* Wickenburg *Miner,* and *Hassayampa Miner*—are on file at the Arizona State Library, at the capitol in Phoenix; however, when last checked, access to these papers was forbidden because of their deteriorating condition. The State Library also has some copies of the *Arizona State Miner,* from 1919 to 1926 (which can be examined), as well as microfilm copies of the *Hassayampa Sun,* later the *Wickenburg Sun,* which began publishing in 1924 and has continued to the present.

Index

Aguila, 73, 123

Arizona and California Railroad, 67

Arizona Gliding Academy, 123–24

Arizona Nature Conservancy, 140–41

Arizona Sampling and Reduction Company, 67

Bachtiger, John, 70

Bar F X Ranch, 98, 99, 100, 101, 102, 108, 114 (photo)

Bass, Bill, 104–5

Bass Pavilion, 105

Bass, William, 104

Baxter Hotel, 68, 88 (photo)

Baxter Opera House, 105, 140

Baxter, R. W., 70

Belmont Hotel, 104

Bicknell, P. C., 58

Brayton Commercial Company, 69, 71, 78 (photo), 80 (photo), 104, 110, 131, 133

Brenda Cutoff, 134

Brill, Frederick, 47, 50, 90, 140

Burden, Dana, 136, 137

Burden, Jack, 98

Burden, Sophie, 96, 108, 122, 130, 135

California and Arizona Stage Company, 49

Castle Hot Springs, 89, 90, 97

Cattle Rustlers Ball, 100

Cervantes, Primativo, 42

Chamberlain, D. S., 25

Circle Flying W Ranch, 99, 108, 135

Civil Works Administration, 110

Claiborne Flight Academy, 124

Claiborne, Henry C., 123

Congress, 62, 71, 109

Congress Junction, 61, 62, 66

Congress Mine, 57, 59, 61–62, 71, 92, 109, 123

Copper Belt, 66

Cowell, Henry, 38 (photo), 70

Coxwell, Roy, 109

Crampton, Frank, 66

Crook, Gen. George, 44–45

Date Creek, Camp, 43, 45
Date Creek reservation, 43–44
Desert Caballeros, 119 (photo),
    128–29
Desert Caballeros Western
    Museum, 132, 133, 140
Diamond P Ranch, 130

Espejo, Antonio de, 9
Eyerly, Lee, 127

Farfán de los Godos, Marcos, 9
First Presbyterian Church, 69, 126
Fletcher, Pete, 93, 130
Flying E Ranch, 127, 129, 130, 138

Gant, Edith and Dallas, 128
Garcés, Francisco, 10
Garcia Cemetery, 55
Garcia Dance Hall, 105
Garcia, Edward L., 70
Garcia, Felipe, 70
Garcia School. See Wickenburg
    Grammar School
Garcia, Ygnacio, 33 (photo), 55, 58,
    69, 78 (photo)
Garden of Allah, 90–91, 97, 99, 135,
    140
Genung, Charles, 21
Gold Rush Days, 111
Groom, Robert, 24

Hall, DeForest (Dick Wick), 68
Hammer, Angela, 35 (photo), 68
Hassayampa Placer Gold Company,
    109
Hassayampa River, 3–5, 11, 18, 23, 24,
    50, 83 (photo), 90, 93, 95, 105, 106,
    110, 140–41

Hassayampa River Preserve, 3–4,
    141
Hot Springs Junction, 90
Howard, Rowena and Belford, 128

James, George Wharton, 72, 75
Jerome Junction, 61
Julian, C. C., 92

Kaiser Gold Mining Company, 53
Kay El Bar Ranch, 98, 99, 100, 108,
    130, 138
Kerr, Donald and Margaret, 127

La Paz, 16
Las Damas, 129
Lazy Fox Ranch, 130
Lazy R C Ranch, 108, 135
Lowdermilk, Romaine, 98, 99

Machan, W. T., 72
MacLennan, H. K., 126
Maguire, Sylvia and C. L. "Squire,"
    128
Maricopa Indians, 6, 8, 12, 41, 46
Matchette, Hazel, 73
M-Bar-V Ranch. See Monte Vista
    Ranch
McPherson, Camp, 43
Monte Cristo Mine, 82 (photo), 92,
    93
Monte Vista Ranch, 99, 100, 101,
    102, 108, 115 (photo), 129, 130
Muchos Canyon, 45
Murphy, Frank, 59, 61, 62, 90

O'Brien, Anthony "Tony," 79
    (photo), 95, 98, 104
O'Brien, Francis X., 103

Octave Mine, 66, 92, 123
Oñate, Don Juan de, 9, 10
Oro Grande Mine, 65, 66, 110

Pay'n Takit, 104
Peeples, Abraham H., 16, 17, 25, 41
Phelps, Behtchuel, 22
Pima Indians, 6, 8, 12, 41
Pioneer Mining District, 17
Prescott & Arizona Central
    Railroad, 59, 61
Prescott, T. J., 70
Priestley, J. B., 111, 112
Pumpkin Patch, 4

Rancho Casitas, 130, 138
Rancho de los Caballeros, 128, 130,
    132, 135, 138
Remuda Ranch, 95, 98–99, 101, 102,
    108, 111, 114 (photo), 122, 123, 128,
    130, 132, 135
Reynolds, Joseph "Diamond Joe,"
    59, 61
Richards, Dad, 110
Rich Hill, 16, 17, 19
Riggs, John, 38 (photo), 70
Rio Verde reservation, 44, 45
Round-Up Club, 111, 117 (photo),
    136
Rusk, Theodore Green, 20, 21
Rusling, Gen. James E., 23, 24, 25

Safeway, 132
San Carlos reservation, 45
Sanger, John and Frances, 90
Santa Fe, Prescott & Phoenix
    Railroad, 60, 62, 67, 140
Santa Fe Railroad, 67, 140
Seymour, 47, 52, 54

Shady River–Palm Lake Guest
    Ranch, 135
Simpson, Aimee Pouquette, 94, 104
Skeleton Cave (Skull Cave), 45
Slash Bar K Ranch, 127, 129, 130, 131
Smith, Elizabeth, 68
Smith, William, 68
Smith's Mill, 47
Sombrero Ranch, 108
St. Anthony of Padua, 68, 77
    (photo), 126
Stanton, Charles, 44
Swilling, John "Jack," 41

Tabor, Horace A. W., 53, 63
Thayer, Ezra, 92
Traders' Bank, 72, 108
Triangle W Ranch, 99, 108, 129, 130

Union Oil Corporation, 137
United Verde Extension Company,
    109
Upton, George B., 65

Valenzuela, Inocensio, 44
Valley National Bank, 126
Van Bibber, E. A., 20, 21
Vernetta Hotel, 68, 69, 71, 81
    (photo), 104, 140
Villa, Ray, 108
Vulture (town), 25
Vulture City, 24
Vulture Mine, 20–22, 24, 25–26, 31
    (photo), 32 (photo), 39, 46–48,
    52–53, 62–65, 92, 109, 123

Walker, Joseph, 17
Walker Mining District, 17, 18–19
Walnut Grove Dam, 34 (photo),
    53–54, 63, 70, 95, 141

Warbasse, Henry, 99

Weaver, 17, 19, 24, 41

Weaver, Leo, 97, 98

Weaver Mining District, 17, 18–19

Weaver, Pauline, 15, 16, 17, 40

Wellik, George and Vi, 127

Wells Fargo, 49

Westpark, 137

Whipple, Fort, 19, 42

White, Lewis C. "Bob," 98, 99, 101, 102, 129

Wickenburg Addition, 67

Wickenburg Chamber of Commerce, 136, 140

Wickenburg Community Hospital, 127

Wickenburg Grammar School, 68, 69, 72, 79 (photo), 140

Wickenburg, Henry, 19–22, 23, 24, 33 (photo), 50, 54, 58, 64, 67, 70, 111

Wickenburg High School District, 103

Wickenburg Inn Tennis and Guest Ranch, 135, 138

Wickenburg Massacre, 44

Wickenburg *Miner*, 35 (photo), 68, 91

Wickenburg Mining District, 21

Wickenburg News-Herald, 68

Widmeyer, C. H., 70

Williams, Charles and Helen, 129

Wilson, Harriet, 68

Wood, Ike B., 70

Woolsey, King, 41–42

Works Progress Administration (WPA), 110

Yarnell, 109

Yavapai Indians, 3, 4, 5–8, 8–12, 13, 15, 23, 25, 27 (photo), 39–40, 40–46, 141

Young, Ewing, 11–12

Credits

All photographs are from the collection of the Desert Caballeros Western Museum except for the following: page 27 (Yavapai wickiup) from the Sharlot Hall Museum Library/Archives, Prescott (no. IN-Y-Z111pc); page 31 (Vulture Mine) from the Arizona Historical Society, Tucson (AHS no. 19088); page 79 (school) and page 37 (José Quesada) from the Ocampo Family Photographs, Chicano Research Collection, Department of Archives and Manuscripts, Arizona State University Libraries, Tempe (nos. SPC 173:42 and SPC 173:863, respectively).

The map was drawn by Ed Byerly.

The Town on the Hassayampa: A History of Wickenburg, Arizona was designed and typeset by Emmy Ezzell in Minion type. The photographs were scanned for reproduction by Land O' Sun Printers. Thomson-Shore, Inc., printed the book on 60# Glatfelter Supple Opaque, an acid-free paper, and bound the softcover edition.

A special hard cover limited edition was also bound by Thomson-Shore.